DEFENSE, SECURITY AND STRATEGIES

AF734453

DEPARTMENT OF DEFENSE CONTRACT OBLIGATIONS

A REVIEW OF HOW AND WHERE MONEY IS SPENT

DEFENSE, SECURITY AND STRATEGIES

Additional books in this series can be found on Nova's website under the Series tab.

Additional e-books in this series can be found on Nova's website under the e-book tab.

DEFENSE, SECURITY AND STRATEGIES

DEPARTMENT OF DEFENSE CONTRACT OBLIGATIONS

A REVIEW OF HOW AND WHERE MONEY IS SPENT

JOSEPH HODSON
EDITOR

NOVINKA
New York

Copyright © 2015 by Nova Science Publishers, Inc.

All rights reserved. No part of this book may be reproduced, stored in a retrieval system or transmitted in any form or by any means: electronic, electrostatic, magnetic, tape, mechanical photocopying, recording or otherwise without the written permission of the Publisher.

We have partnered with Copyright Clearance Center to make it easy for you to obtain permissions to reuse content from this publication. Simply navigate to this publication's page on Nova's website and locate the "Get Permission" button below the title description. This button is linked directly to the title's permission page on copyright.com. Alternatively, you can visit copyright.com and search by title, ISBN, or ISSN.

For further questions about using the service on copyright.com, please contact:
Copyright Clearance Center
Phone: +1-(978) 750-8400 Fax: +1-(978) 750-4470 E-mail: info@copyright.com.

NOTICE TO THE READER

The Publisher has taken reasonable care in the preparation of this book, but makes no expressed or implied warranty of any kind and assumes no responsibility for any errors or omissions. No liability is assumed for incidental or consequential damages in connection with or arising out of information contained in this book. The Publisher shall not be liable for any special, consequential, or exemplary damages resulting, in whole or in part, from the readers' use of, or reliance upon, this material. Any parts of this book based on government reports are so indicated and copyright is claimed for those parts to the extent applicable to compilations of such works.

Independent verification should be sought for any data, advice or recommendations contained in this book. In addition, no responsibility is assumed by the publisher for any injury and/or damage to persons or property arising from any methods, products, instructions, ideas or otherwise contained in this publication.

This publication is designed to provide accurate and authoritative information with regard to the subject matter covered herein. It is sold with the clear understanding that the Publisher is not engaged in rendering legal or any other professional services. If legal or any other expert assistance is required, the services of a competent person should be sought. FROM A DECLARATION OF PARTICIPANTS JOINTLY ADOPTED BY A COMMITTEE OF THE AMERICAN BAR ASSOCIATION AND A COMMITTEE OF PUBLISHERS.

Additional color graphics may be available in the e-book version of this book.

Library of Congress Cataloging-in-Publication Data

ISBN: 978-1-63483-768-2

Published by Nova Science Publishers, Inc. † New York

CONTENTS

PREFACE

The Department of Defense (DOD) has long relied on contractors to provide the U.S. military with a wide range of goods and services, including weapons, food, uniforms, and operational support. Without contractor support, the United States would be currently unable to arm and field an effective fighting force. Understanding costs and trends associated with contractor support could provide Congress more information upon which to make budget decisions and weigh the relative costs and benefits of different military operations—including contingency operations and maintaining bases around the world. Obligations occur when agencies enter into contracts, employ personnel, or otherwise commit to spending money. The federal government tracks money obligated on federal contracts through a database called the Federal Procurement Data System-Next Generation (FPDS). There is no public database that tracks DOD contract outlays (money spent) as comprehensively as obligations. This book examines how much money DOD obligates on contracts; what DOD is buying; and where that money is being spent. This book also examines the extent to which these data are sufficiently reliable to use as a factor when developing policy or analyzing government operations. In addition, this book provides background information and identifies issues for Congress on the use of contractors to support military operations. DOD's extensive use of contractors poses several potential policy and oversight issues for Congress and has been the focus of numerous hearings. Congress' decisions on these issues could substantially affect the extent to which DOD relies on contractors in and is capable of planning for and overseeing contractors in future operations.

In: Department of Defense Contract Obligations ISBN: 978-1-63483-768-2
Editor: Joseph Hodson © 2015 Nova Science Publishers, Inc.

Chapter 1

DEFENSE ACQUISITIONS: HOW AND WHERE DOD SPENDS ITS CONTRACTING DOLLARS*

Moshe Schwartz, Wendy Ginsberg and John F. Sargent Jr.

SUMMARY

The Department of Defense (DOD) has long relied on contractors to provide the U.S. military with a wide range of goods and services, including weapons, food, uniforms, and operational support. Without contractor support, the United States would be currently unable to arm and field an effective fighting force. Understanding costs and trends associated with contractor support could provide Congress more information upon which to make budget decisions and weigh the relative costs and benefits of different military operations—including contingency operations and maintaining bases around the world.

Obligations occur when agencies enter into contracts, employ personnel, or otherwise commit to spending money. The federal government tracks money obligated on federal contracts through a database called the Federal Procurement Data System-Next Generation (FPDS). There is no public database that tracks DOD contract outlays (money spent) as comprehensively as obligations.

* This is an edited, reformatted and augmented version of a Congressional Research Service publication R44010, prepared for Members and Committees of Congress, dated April 30, 2015.

Total DOD Contract Obligations

In FY2014, DOD obligated more money on federal contracts ($285 billion) than all other government agencies combined. DOD's obligations were equal to 8% of federal spending. Services accounted for 45% of total DOD contract obligations, goods for 45%, and research and development (R&D) for 10%. This distribution is in contrast to the rest of the federal government, which obligated a significantly larger portion of contracting dollars on services (68%), than on goods (22%) or research and development (9%).

According to FPDS data, from FY2000 to FY2014, DOD contract obligations increased from $190 billion to $290 billion (FY2015 dollars). However, the increase in spending has not been steady. DOD contract obligations over the last 15 years are marked by a steep increase of $260 billion from FY2000 to FY2008 (averaging 11% annual increases), followed by a substantial drop of $160 billion (averaging 7% annual decreases) from FY2008 to FY2014. This boom-and-bust trend of DOD contract obligations, which makes budget cutting more difficult due to relatively large budget swings, is in marked contrast to the rest of the federal government, which has had more gradual increases and less drastic contract spending cuts.

For almost 20 years, DOD has dedicated an ever-smaller share of its contracting dollars to R&D, with such contracts dropping from 18% of total contract obligations in FY1998 to 10% in FY2014.

Understanding the Limitation of FPDS Data

Decision-makers should be cautious when using obligation data from FPDS to develop policy or otherwise draw conclusions. In some cases, the data itself may not be reliable. For example, according to DOD officials, the data in FPDS over-represents FY2008 obligations by $13 billion and under-represents FY2009 obligations by the same amount. Depending on the query, understanding and pulling reports from FPDS can be confusing and difficult to interpret. In some instances, a query for particular data may return differing results, depending on the type of query used.

Despite the limitations of FPDS, imperfect data is sometimes better than no data. A number of foreign observers have noted that despite its shortcomings, FPDS data is substantially better than what is available in virtually any other country in the world. FPDS data can be used to identify some broad trends and rough estimations, or to gather information about specific contracts. Understanding the limitations of data—knowing when, how, and to what extent to rely on data— could help policymakers incorporate FPDS data more effectively into their decision-making process.

GSA is undertaking a multi-year effort to improve the reliability and usefulness of the information contained in FPDS and other federal government information systems. This effort, if successful, could significantly improve DOD's ability to engage in evidence- and data-based decision-making.

This report examines (1) how much money DOD obligates on contracts, (2) what DOD is buying, and (3) where that money is being spent. This report also examines the extent to which these data are sufficiently reliable to use as a factor when developing policy or analyzing government operations.

INTRODUCTION

The Department of Defense (DOD) has long relied on contractors to provide the U.S. military with a wide range of goods and services, including weapons, food, uniforms, and operational support. Without contractor support, the United States would currently be unable to arm and field an effective fighting force. Understanding costs and trends associated with contractor support could provide Congress more information upon which to make budget decisions and weigh the relative costs and benefits of different military operations—including contingency operations and maintaining bases around the world.

This report examines (1) how much money DOD obligates on contracts, (2) what DOD is buying, and (3) where that money is being spent. This report also examines the extent to which these data are sufficiently reliable to use as a factor when developing policy or analyzing government operations.

DOD CONTRACT OBLIGATIONS

When Congress appropriates money, it provides *budget authority*—the authority to enter into obligations. *Obligations* occur when agencies enter into contracts, submit purchase orders, employ personnel, or otherwise legally commit to spending money. *Outlays* occur when obligations are liquidated (primarily through the issuance of checks, electronic fund transfers, or the disbursement of cash).[1]

How Are Government Contract Data Tracked?

The Federal Procurement Data System—Next Generation (FPDS) is a central database of U.S. government-wide procurement. The purpose of FPDS is to provide data that can be used as "a basis for recurring and special reports to the President, the Congress, the Government Accountability Office, Federal executive agencies, and the general public."[2] The contract data in this report come from the FPDS database.

FPDS generally reports information on contracts that exceed $3,000 in obligations.[3] FPDS-NG does not include data from judicial branch agencies, the legislative branch, certain DOD components, or select executive branch agencies—such as the Central Intelligence Agency and National Security Agency.[4] FPDS lists data from GAO.[5] Unless otherwise indicated, all data in this report is derived from FPDS.

Due to concerns over data reliability (see below), data from FPDS are used in this report to identify broad trends and rough estimations. FPDS contains data from 1978 to the present. For a more detailed discussion on how FPDS operates, see Appendix A.

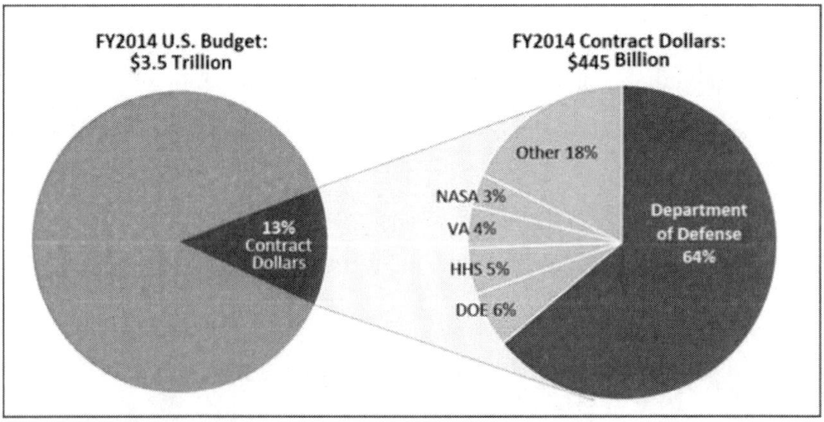

Source: Federal Procurement Data System-Next Generation, January 2015. Figure created by CRS.

Figure 1. Contract Obligations by Agency.

In FY2014, the U.S. federal government obligated $445 billion for contracts for the acquisition of goods, services, and research and development. The $445 billion obligated on contracts was equal to approximately 13% of FY2014 federal budget outlays of $3.5 trillion.[6] As noted in Figure 1, in FY2014, DOD obligated more money on federal contracts ($284 billion) than all other federal agencies combined. DOD's obligations were equal to 8% of federal spending.

From FY2000 to FY2014, adjusted for inflation (FY2015 dollars), DOD contract obligations increased from $189 billion to $290 billion.[7] However, the increase in spending has not been steady. Over the last 15 years, DOD contracting has been marked by a steep increase in obligations from FY2000 to FY2008 ($260 billion; 138%), followed by a substantial drop in obligations ($160 billion; 35%) from FY2008 to FY2014 (see Figure 2).

Contract obligation trends are generally consistent with overall DOD obligation trends. For example, DOD total obligation authority increased significantly from FY2000 to FY2008, and decreased from FY2008 to FY2014 (see Figure 3).

Some analysts believe that this trend of rapid contract spending increases (averaging 11% annual increases), followed by a relatively sharp cut in contract spending (averaging 7% annual decreases), puts DOD at increased risk of making short-term budget decisions (aimed at meeting budget caps) that could cause long-term harm. These analysts argue that, even without changing long-term budget reduction targets, DOD should make more strategically informed decisions.[8]

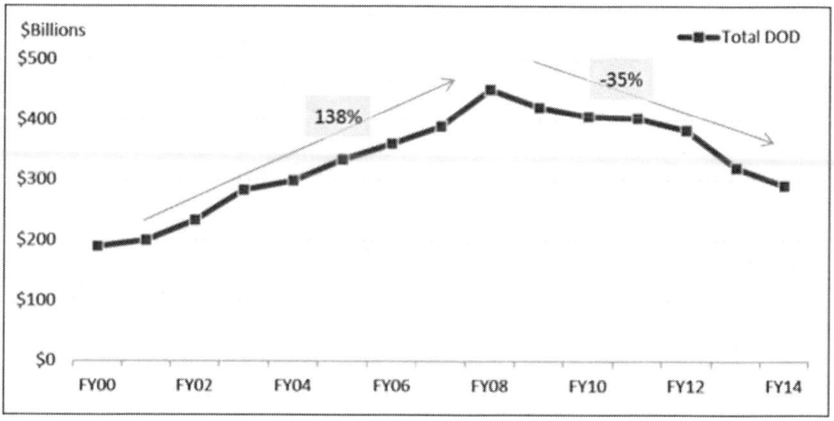

Source: CRS analysis of data from the Federal Procurement Data System—Next Generation, January 2015. Figure created by CRS.

Figure 2. DOD Contract Obligations. (FY2015 Dollars)

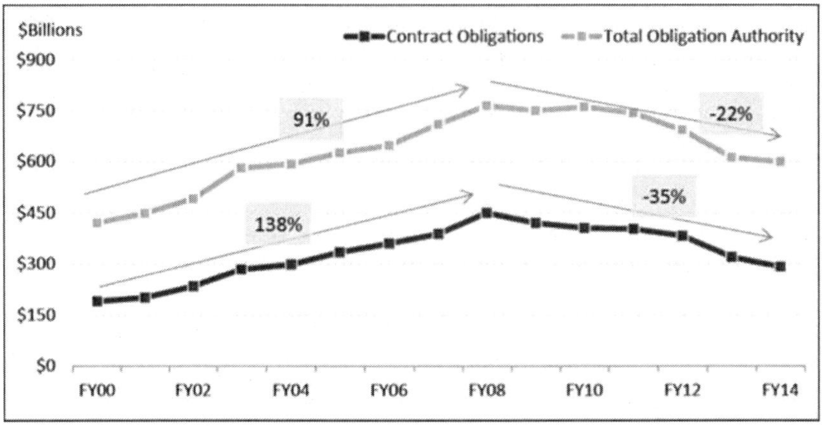

Source: Office of the Under Secretary of Defense (Comptroller), Department of Defense, National Defense Budget Estimates for FY2016, "Department of Defense TOA – By Public Title," Table 6-1, March, 2015. Figure created by CRS.

Figure 3. DOD—Total Obligation Authority. (FY2015 Dollars)

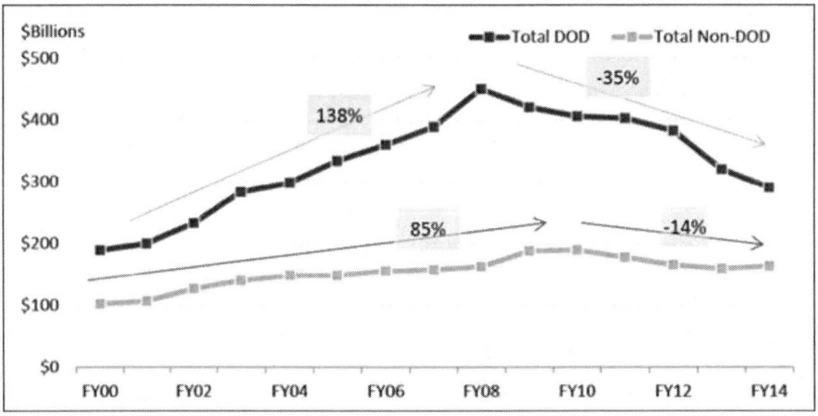

Source: CRS analysis of FPDS data. Figure created by CRS.

Figure 4. DOD vs. Rest of Government Contract Obligations. (FY2015 Dollars)

The limits on DOD funding resulting from the Budget Control Act could result in cuts that are not strategically thought out.[9] A more gradual reduction in spending, or additional funding in select budget categories, could help DOD make more gradual spending reductions and more considered choices, potentially minimizing hazardous long-term effects of budget cuts. Addressing budget cuts, former Pentagon comptroller Robert Hale wrote that one option for Congress is to

> approve more funding in at least some budget categories and raise the budget caps to accommodate the boosted funding. This could be accomplished in a mini budget deal (as opposed to the forever elusive "grand bargain") that, hopefully for at least a few years, would effectively eliminate the threat of sequestration in favor of *considered choices* (italics added).[10]

The boom-and-bust trend of DOD contract spending that makes budget cuts more difficult is in marked contrast to the rest of the federal government, which has had more gradual increases and less drastic spending cuts (see Figure 4).

What DOD Is Buying

In FY2014, 45% of total DOD contract obligations were for services, 45% for goods, and 10% for research and development (R&D). This is in contrast to the rest of the federal government (excluding DOD), which obligated a significantly larger portion of contracting dollars on services (68%) than on goods (22%) or research and development (9%).

How Are Contracts Categorized?

FPDS categorizes contracts by product or service codes. According to FPDS, "These product/service codes are used to record the products and services being purchased by the Federal Government. In many cases, a given contract/task order/purchase order will include more than one product and/or service. In such cases, the product or service code data element code should be selected based on the predominant product or service that is being purchased. For example, a contract for $1000 of lumber and $500 of pipe would be coded under 5510, Lumber & Related Wood Materials."

Because FPDS-NG contracts are associated with only a single product or service code—even when the contract involves substantial deliveries of other products or services—the analysis in this report should be used only to identify broad overall trends.

Source: U.S. General Services Administration Office of Governmentwide Policy, Federal Procurement Data System Product and Service Codes Manual, August 2011 Edition, October 1, 2011, p. 6.

For almost 20 years, DOD has dedicated an ever-smaller share of contracting dollars to R&D, with such contracts dropping from 18% of total contract obligations in FY1998 to 10% in FY2014. (For a breakout of DOD obligations trends by product service code, see Appendix B.)

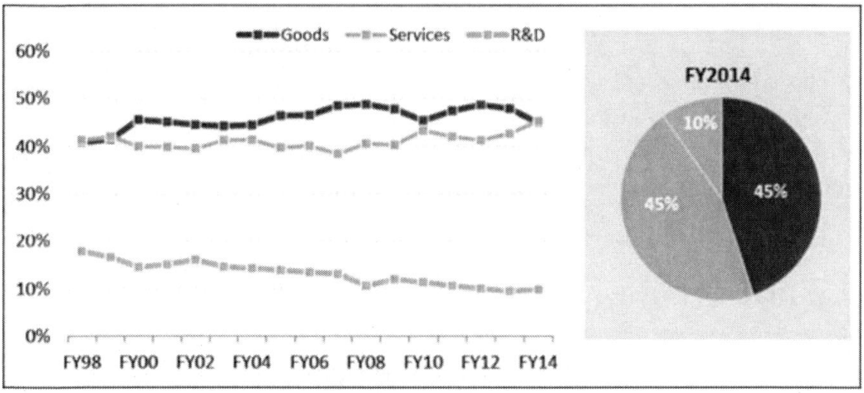

Source: CRS analysis of FPDS data. Figure created by CRS.

Figure 5. DOD Contract Obligations by Major Category.

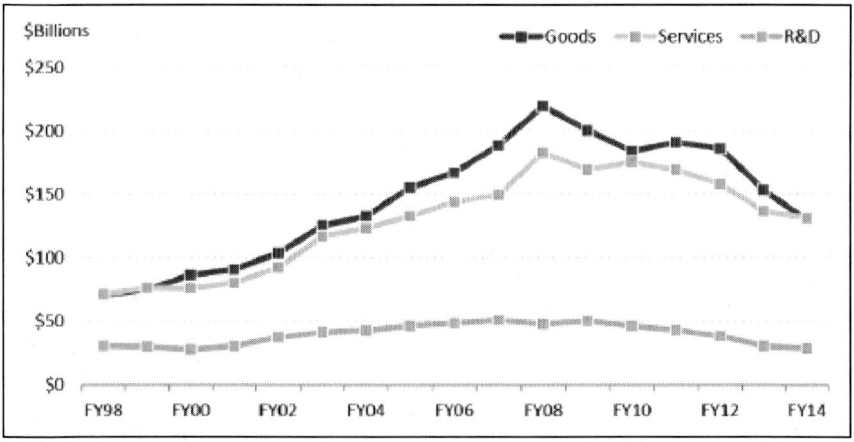

Source: CRS analysis of FPDS data. Figure created by CRS.

Figure 6. DOD Contract Obligations Dedicated to R&D. (FY2015 Dollars)

The relative decrease in R&D contracts is not just as a percentage of overall spending, but also in terms of constant dollars. Despite increased spending on R&D from FY2000 to FY2007, adjusted for inflation, DOD obligated less money on R&D contracts in FY2014 ($28 billion) than it invested more than 15 years earlier ($31 billion in FY1998). In contrast, over the same period, DOD obligations to acquire both goods and services are substantially higher than they were 15 years ago (see Figure 6).

Total DOD Spending on Research, Development, Test, and Evaluation (RDT&E)

Research and Development contracting is but a portion of overall DOD investment in developing technology. For example, more than half of DOD's basic research budget is spent at universities and represents the major contribution of funds in some areas of science and technology.[11] When taken as a whole, the R&D picture looks somewhat different. Total outlays for RDT&E[12] increased 70% in constant dollars from FY1998 to FY2009, before dropping 24% from FY2009 to FY2014.[13] However, as reflected in Figure 7, over the last 15 years, RDT&E outlays increased at a much slower rate (30%) than non-RDT&E (54%).

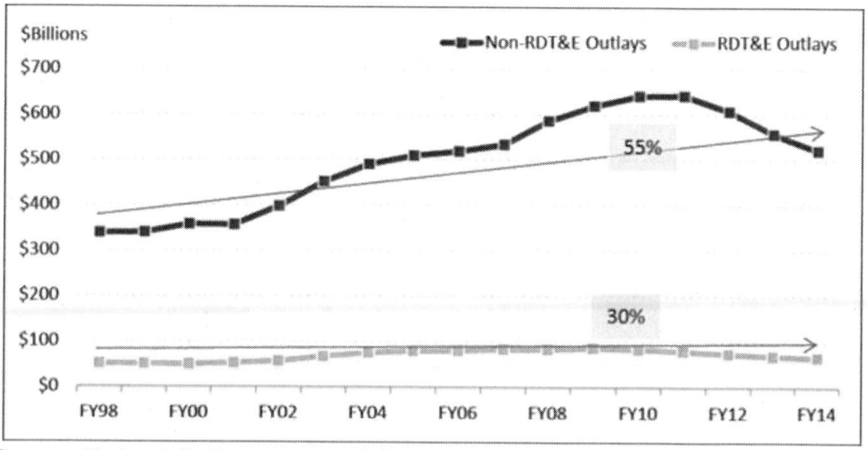

Source: National Defense Budget Estimates for FY 2015, Department of Defense Outlays by Public Title, Table 6-11. Figure created by CRS. FY2014 data from National Defense Budget Estimates for FY 2016, Department of Defense Outlays by Public Title, Table 6-11.

Figure 7. DOD RDT&E vs. Non-RDT&E Outlays. (FY2015 Dollars)

The Global Environment for R&D

The profile of DOD R&D spending takes place against a backdrop of increasing defense and nondefense investments by foreign nations and private industry. As reflected in Figure 8, U.S. federal defense-related R&D dropped from 36% of global R&D in 1960 to 7% in 1998, and to 5% in 2012.

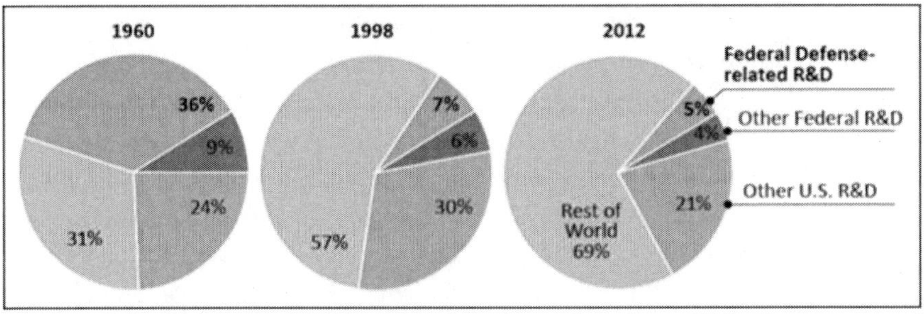

Source: 1960: U.S. and ROW shares based on data from U.S. Department of Commerce, Office of Technology Policy, The Global Context for U.S. Technology Policy, Summer 1997 (hard copy). 2012: U.S. and ROW share from OECD, Main Science and Technology Indicators, OECD. Stat. Figure created by CRS.

Figure 8. Comparison of R&D Spending 1960-2012.

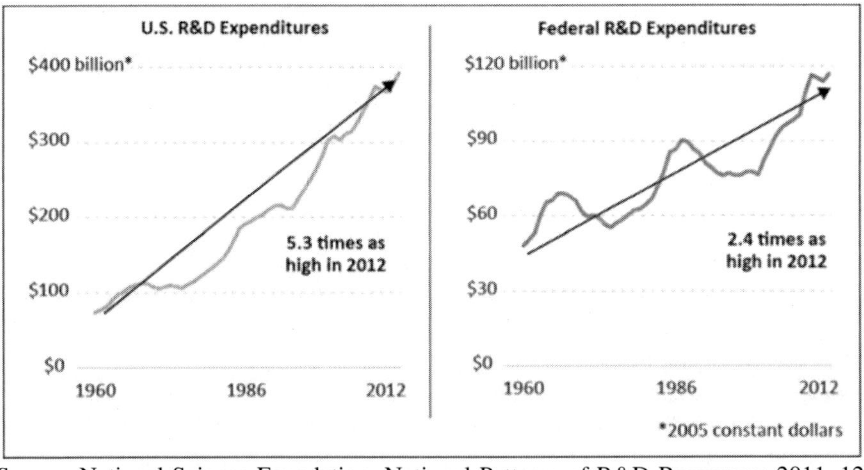

Source: National Science Foundation, National Patterns of R&D Resources: 2011–12 Data Update, NSF 14-304, Table 6, December 2013, at http://nsf.gov/statistics/nsf14304/. Figure created by CRS.

Figure 9. Federal and U.S. Expenditures.

The reduction in U.S. and federal government shares of global R&D did not result from decreased U.S. spending, but from the increased R&D spending of other nations in aggregate. In constant dollars, federal R&D

funding in 2012 was 2.4 times its 1960 level, while total U.S. R&D funding in 2012 was 5.3 times its 1960 level (see Figure 9).

In recent years, China has increased its R&D expenditures at a rapid pace to become the second-largest funder of R&D among nations. Figure 10 shows growth in R&D expenditures for selected nations since 2000, as reported to the OECD, and illustrates the comparatively rapid growth of China's R&D investments with respect to those of other nations.

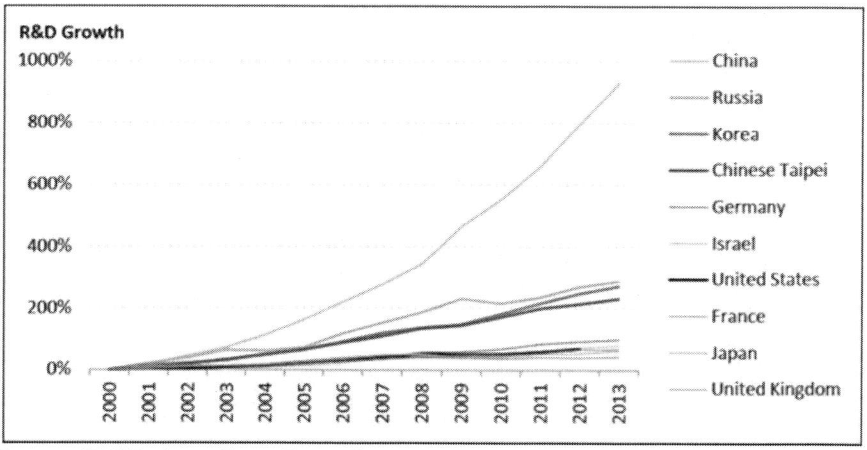

Source: OECD data, Gross Expenditures on R&D (GERD), 2012. Figure created by CRS. (China is the top line).

Figure 10. Growth in Gross Expenditures on R&D for Selected Nations Since 2000.

While the growth shown in Figure 10 is for total R&D funding, these trends have raised concerns among many analysts and senior DOD leaders, such as Under Secretary of Defense Frank Kendall, who testified in January 2015 that

> [O]ver the past few decades, the U.S. and our allies have enjoyed a military capability advantage over any potential adversary.... The First Gulf War put this suite of technologies and the associated operational concepts on display for the world to observe and study. The First Gulf War also marked the beginning of a period of American military dominance that has lasted about a quarter of a century and served us well in several conflicts. We used the same capabilities, with some notable enhancements, in Serbia, Afghanistan, Libya and Iraq. It has been a good run, but the game isn't one sided, and all military advantages based on technology are temporary... .

> The rise of foreign capability, coupled with the overall decline in U.S. research and development investments, is jeopardizing our technological superiority.[14]

The United States remains the world's single largest funder of R&D, spending more than the next two highest funders combined (China and Japan) in 2012 (see Table 1). Global R&D is highly concentrated among a few nations. The 10 nations listed in Table 1 accounted for more than 80% of global R&D reported to the OECD in 2012.

Table 1. Total 2012 Gross Expenditures on R&D, by Nation in billions of current purchasing power parity (PPP) U.S. dollars

Nation	Amount
United States	$453.5
China	293.1
Japan	151.8
Germany	100.7
South Korea	64.5
France	55.5
United Kingdom	38.9
Russian Federation	38.8
Chinese Taipei	28.7
Italy	26.9

Source: CRS analysis of OECD website data, Gross Expenditures on R&D (GERD), 2012.

Notes: Purchasing power parity is an economic analysis tool used to adjust international currencies to a common currency (in this case, U.S. dollars) based on each currency's domestic purchasing power.

Michael Dumont, Principal Deputy Assistant Secretary of Defense for Special Operations/Low Intensity Conflict, reportedly stated

> Many of our adversaries have acquired, developed and even stolen technologies that have put them on somewhat equal footing with the West in a range of areas... the U.S. government no longer has the leading edge developing its own leading edge capabilities, particularly in information technology.[15]

In the early 1960s, the federal government funded approximately twice as much R&D as U.S. industry and thus played a substantial role in driving U.S. and global technology pathways. Today, U.S. industry funds more than twice as much R&D as the federal government. This transformation has had, and continues to have, implications for federal R&D strategy and management and for the efficacy of the DOD acquisition system. As one general officer stated, whereas the military used to go to industry and tell them to create a technology to meet a requirement, increasingly the military is going to industry and asking them to adapt an existing commercial technology to military requirements.[16]

Where DOD Obligates Contract Dollars

DOD relies on contractors to support operations worldwide, including operations in Afghanistan, permanently garrisoned troops overseas, and ships docking at foreign ports. Because of its global footprint, this report will look at where DOD obligates contract dollars in two ways:

1. by geographic region.
2. domestic vs. overseas.

What Is Place of Performance?

FPDS defines place of performance as "the location of the principal plant or place of business where the items will be produced, supplied from stock, or where the service will be performed."[17] Foreign place of performance is defined here as work produced, supplied, or performed primarily outside of the United States or its territories.

According to DOD, the FPDS is required to collect only the predominant place of performance for contract actions. Because FPDS lists only one country for place of performance, contracts listed as being performed in one country can also involve substantial performance in other countries. In 2012, GAO noted that FPDS's inability to provide more granular data entry and analysis limited the "utility, accuracy, and completeness" of the data.[18]

By Geographic Region

DOD divides its missions and geographic responsibilities among six unified combatant commands:

1) U.S. Northern Command (NORTHCOM),[19]
2) U.S. African Command (AFRICOM),
3) U.S. Central Command (CENTCOM),[20]
4) U.S. European Command (EUCOM),
5) U.S. Pacific Command (PACOM), which includes Hawaii and a number of U.S. territories,[21] and
6) U.S. Southern Command (SOUTHCOM).[22]

These commands do not control all DOD contracting activity that occurs within their respective geographic regions. For example, Transportation Command (TRANSCOM), headquartered at Scott Air Force Base, IL, may contract with a private company to provide transportation services in CENTCOM. For purposes of this report, DOD contract obligations are categorized by the place of performance, not the DOD component that signed the contract or obligated the money. For example, all contract obligations for work in the geographic location that falls under the responsibility of CENTCOM will be allocated to CENTCOM, regardless of which DOD organization signed the contract.

In FY2014, 90% of DOD contracts were performed in NORTHCOM (which includes the Bahamas, Canada, and Mexico). DOD obligated 4% of total contract work in CENTCOM, followed by PACOM (2.5%), EUCOM (2%), AFRICOM (0.17%), and SOUTHCOM (0.14%).

Domestic vs. Overseas

In FY2014, 92% of DOD contract obligations ($265 billion in FY2015 dollars) were for work performed in the United States, the highest percentage since FY2003 (see Figure 11).[23] Over the last six years, obligations for domestic contracts dropped by 34%, from a high of approximately $400 billion in FY2008 to some $265 billion in FY2014; obligations for overseas contracts were cut in half, from $48 billion in FY2008 to $24 billion in FY2014. The drop in overseas obligations stems primarily from drawdowns in the Iraq and Afghanistan theaters, where contract obligations decreased from $32.5 billion in FY2008 to $12.5 billion in FY2014 (Figure 12).[24]

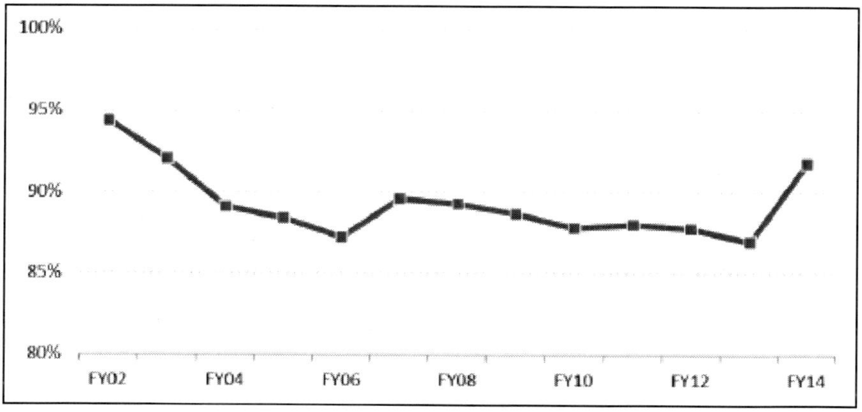

Source: CRS analysis of FPDS data. Figure created by CRS.

Figure 11. Percentage of DOD Contract Obligations Performed in the United States.

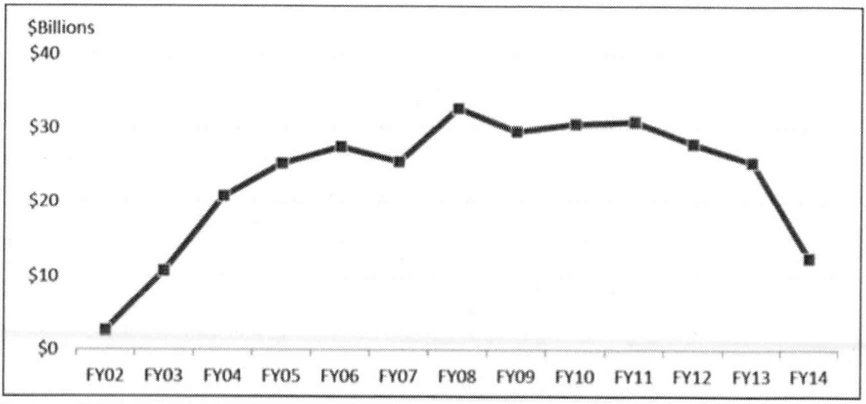

Source: CRS Analysis of FPDS data. Figure created by CRS.

Figure 12. Contract Obligations in Iraq and Afghanistan Theaters. (FY2015 Dollars)

Despite the drawdown in Iraq and Afghanistan, in FY2014 DOD contract obligations for work performed overseas were still primarily steered to CENTCOM (52%), followed by EUCOM (21%), PACOM (18%), NORTHCOM (6%), SOUTHCOM (2%), and AFRICOM (2%) (Figure 13). However, a significant shift in where contracting dollars are allocated appears to be underway. Fewer dollars are being obligated in CENTCOM and EUCOM, whereas more dollars are being directed toward PACOM (see Table 2).

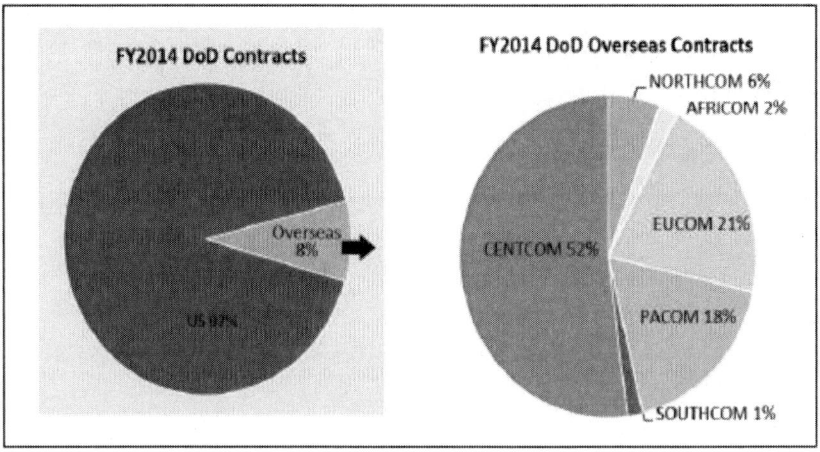

Source: CRS Analysis of FPDS data. Figure created by CRS.

Figure 13. DOD Contract Obligations for Work Performed in Combatant Command Areas of Responsibility.

Table 2. Obligations for Contracts Performed Overseas FY2015 Dollars

Unified Combatant Command[a]	FY2008	FY2014	Change
CENTCOM	$32,783,702,635	$12,483,406,051	-62%
EUCOM	$10,440,264,437	$4,987,819,112	-52%
PACOM	$2,983,932,444	$4,236,333,879	42%
NORTHCOM	$1,329,916,478	$1,376,759,556	4%
AFRICOM	$312,105,190	$493,098,812	58%
SOUTHCOM	$416,188,774	$396,447,846	-5%

Source: CRS Analysis of FPDS data, January, 2015.

Note: FY2008 chosen as point of comparison because FY2008 is the high point of DOD contract obligations.

[a] Does not include contracts performed in the United States and its territories.

Of the top 12 countries where DOD contractors perform work abroad, 5 were in CENTCOM, 3 in EUCOM, 2 in PACOM, and 2 in NORTHCOM (see Appendix C).

DOD Overseas Obligations vs. Rest of Government

DOD's share of total government obligations for contracts performed abroad has trended down from a high of 90% in FY2000 to 71% in FY2014. Over the same period, combined Department of State and USAID contract obligations increased from 4% to 24% of all U.S. government overseas obligations (see Figure 14).

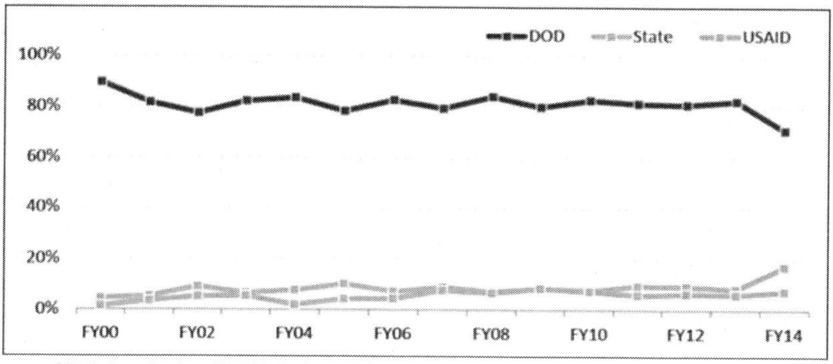

Source: CRS Analysis of FPDS data. Figure created by CRS.

Notes: USAID was established as an independent agency in 1961, but receives overall foreign policy guidance from the Secretary of State.

Figure 14. DOD's Proportion of Total U.S. Government Contract Work Performed Overseas.

A number of analysts have argued that as a result of its larger budget and workforce, DOD often undertakes traditionally civilian missions because other agencies do not have the necessary resources to fulfill those missions.[25] Some of these analysts argue that more resources should be invested into civilian agencies to allow them to play a larger role in conflict prevention, post-conflict stabilization, and reconstruction. As The Senate Foreign Relations Committee Majority, Discussion Paper on Peacekeeping, Majority Staff, April 8, 2010, stated, "The civilian capacity of the U.S. Government to prevent conflict and conduct post-conflict stabilization and reconstruction is beset by fragmentation, gaps in coverage, lack of resources and training, coordination problems, unclear delineations of authority and responsibility, and policy inconsistency."

Many of these analysts have argued that to achieve its foreign policy goals, the United States needs to take a more whole-of-government approach that brings together the resources of, among others, DOD, the Department of State, and USAID—and government contractors. Then-Secretary of Defense Robert Gates echoed this approach when he argued, in 2007, for strengthening the use of soft power in national security through increased nondefense spending. As Secretary Gates stated:

> What is clear to me is that there is a need for a dramatic increase in spending on the civilian instruments of national security—diplomacy, strategic communications, foreign assistance, civic action, and economic reconstruction and development.... We must focus our energies beyond the guns and steel of the military, beyond just our brave soldiers, sailors, Marines, and airmen. We must also focus our energies on the other elements of national power that will be so crucial in the coming years.[26]

Contract obligations since FY2000 may indicate a shift toward a more whole-of-government approach to achieving foreign policy objectives.

How Reliable Are the DOD Data on Contract Obligations?

According to the Federal Acquisition Regulation, FPDS-NG can be used to measure and assess "the effect of Federal contracting on the Nation's economy and ... the effect of other policy and management initiatives (e.g., performance based acquisitions and competition)."[27] FPDS is also used to meet the requirements of the Federal Funding Accountability and Transparency Act of 2006 (P.L. 109-282), which requires all federal award data to be publicly accessible.

Congress, legislative and executive branch agencies, analysts, and the public all rely on FPDS as a primary source of information for understanding how and where the federal government spends contracting dollars. Congress and the executive branch rely on the information to help make and oversee informed policy and spending decisions. Analysts and the public rely on the data in FPDS to conduct analysis and gain visibility into government operations.

Data reliability is essential to the utility of FPDS. As GAO has stated, "[R]eliable information is critical to informed decision making and to oversight of the procurement system."[28] According to officials within the White House's Office of Federal Procurement Policy, "[c]omplete, accurate, and timely federal procurement data are essential for ensuring that the government has the right information when planning and awarding contracts and that the public has reliable data to track how tax dollars are being spent."[29] If the data contained in FPDS are not sufficiently reliable, the data may not provide an appropriate basis for measuring or assessing federal contracting, making policy decisions, or providing transparency into government operations. The result could be the implementation of policies that squander resources and waste taxpayer dollars. According to GAO, "[f]ederal agencies are responsible for ensuring that the information reported in [the FPDS] dababase is complete and accurate."

Data Reliability Concerns Persist

According to GSA, data in FPDS are provided by agencies and the agencies are required to validate their data annually through the FPDS Data Independent Verification and Validation and Quality Certification. Agency statements regarding data accuracy are independent of the FPDS systems and outside the authority of GSA.

GAO has repeatedly raised concerns over the accuracy, limitations, and reliability of the data contained in the FPDS-NG database.[30] According to GAO, FPDS-NG often contains data with limited "utility, accuracy, and completeness."[31] The Office of Management and Budget has also released guidance requiring executive branch agencies to implement GAO recommendations seeking to improve FPDS data quality.[32] Continued concerns raised over the reliability of data have prompted many analysts to rely on FPDS-NG primarily to identify broad trends and make rough estimations. According to one GAO report:

> DOD acknowledged that using FPDS-NG as the main data source for the inventories has a number of limitations. These limitations include that FPDS-NG does not provide the number of contractor FTEs performing each service, identify the requiring activity, or allow for the identification of all services being procured.[33]

Officials from the General Services Administration, the agency that administers FPDS-NG, stated that data errors in FPDS-NG do not substantively alter the larger context of 1.4 million actions and billions of dollars of obligations entered into the system by DOD every year. Officials have also indicated that whenever possible and feasible, steps are taken to improve the reliability and integrity of the data contained in FPDS. For example, in FY2011, the Congressional Research Service reported on specific data reliability concerns regarding contracts listed as having been performed overseas that were actually performed in the United States.[34] DOD addressed the data error by reviewing past data and correcting coding errors.[35] To prevent similar coding errors in the future, a rule change was implemented requiring agencies to adopt three-letter International Standard (ISO) codes when coding a particular country into FPDS-NG.[36]

Other data deficiencies appear more consequential. According to DOD officials, the obligations for FY2008 are "artificially higher by $13B and the FY09 number is artificially lower by $13B" due to over-obligation on a single contract. DOD went on to note that the money obligated in FY2008 was never spent and that "this is a known error and even had a note in FPDS for a while."[37] Such an error, particularly without an easily identifiable notation, significantly affects analyses of DOD spending trends, including the analysis in this report.

In a more recent example of data inconsistency within FPDS, CRS identified a discrepancy of approximately $6 billion in FY2014 when users employed different methods to extract data from the FPDS database. Although the two methods presumably access the same dataset, in some cases when data were extracted using the system's "standard report," it produced a total dollar value significantly lower than that extracted when using the system's "ad hoc report." The reason for the data discrepancy appears to be that in cases when an agency does not report the place of performance of the contract, the "standard report" omits the contract from search results entirely.[38]

When asked about this particular data discrepancy, GSA stated that the difference was a "feature of the data."[39] CRS extracted FPDS data via both the "standard report" and the "ad hoc report" for all fiscal years available and calculated the resulting discrepancies over time. Figure 15 shows the dollar value of the discrepancy between the two search methods.

Despite the limitations of FPDS, imperfect data are sometimes better than no data. A number of observers have noted that despite its shortcomings, FPDS is one of the world's leading systems for tracking government procurement data.[40] FPDS data can be used to identify some broad trends and rough estimations, or to gather information about specific contracts. Understanding the limitations of data—knowing when, how, and to what extent to rely on data—could help policymakers incorporate FPDS data more effectively into their decision-making process.

GSA Efforts to Improve FPDS

According to GSA, a number of data systems, including FPDS, are undergoing a significant overhaul. This overhaul is a multi-year process that is expected to improve the reliability and usefulness of the information contained in the data systems. Part of the effort includes focus groups with stakeholders, including agency decision-makers and congressional staff, to solicit feedback on how to improve the reliability, usability, and relevance of the data stored in the systems being updated. CRS analysts participated in focus groups. While no date has been set for completing this effort, officials believe that the upgrades will be rolled out sometime in 2017 or 2018.

The extent to which GSA and federal agencies succeed in their efforts to improve the accuracy, reliability, and usability of FPDS will determine the extent to which Congress and senior executive branch officials will have access to reliable and timely data that can be used to make budget and policy decisions.

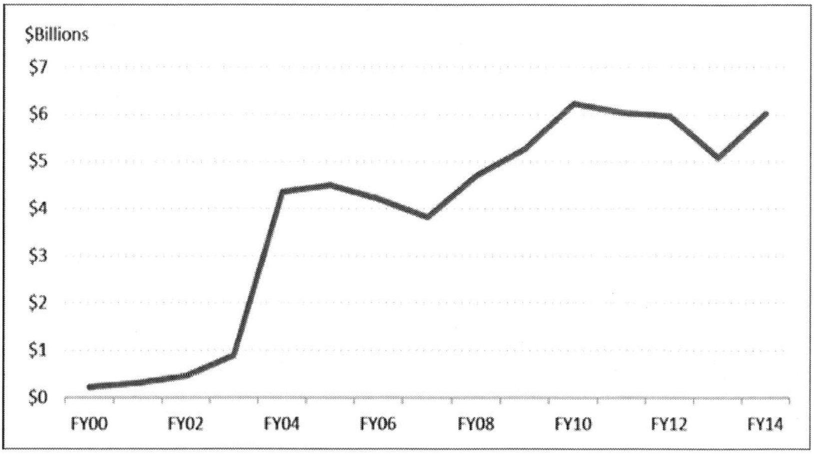

Source: CRS analysis of FPDS data.

Notes: The discrepancy occurs when a user searches for total contracting obligations and requests that the online system sort the data by the place in which the contract was performed. In some cases, when a user employs the "standard report," option within the database, the search yields a lower result than when a user employs the "ad hoc report." Both reports, however, presumably access the same underlying data source to produce their results. The reason for the data discrepancy appears to be that in cases when an agency does not report the place of performance of the contract, the "standard report" omits the contract from search results entirely.

Figure 15. Discrepancy in Different Methods for Calculating Total Contracts Obligations. (Not adjusted for inflation)

APPENDIX A. THE FEDERAL PROCUREMENT DATA SYSTEM

On August 30, 1974, Congress enacted the Office of Federal Procurement Policy Act, which established an Office of Federal Procurement Policy

(OFPP) within the Office of Management and Budget (OMB) and required the establishment of "a system for collecting, developing, and disseminating procurement data which takes into account the needs of Congress, the executive branch, and the private sector."[41] One of the goals of establishing a system for tracking procurement data was to "promote economy, efficiency, and effectiveness in the procurement of property and services."[42]

In February 1978, the OFPP issued a government-wide memorandum that designated the Department of Defense as the executive agent to operate the Federal Procurement Data System.[43] Agencies were instructed to begin collection of procurement data on October 1, 1978, and to report the data to DOD in February 1979.[44] Since 1982, the General Services Administration has operated the system on behalf of the OFPP.[45] Today, FPDS is the only government-wide, publicly available system that contains all federal procurement data. FDPS data are used by other federal-spending information resources, including *USASpending.gov*.

Almost from FPDS's inception, the Government Accountability Office expressed concerns about the accuracy of the information in the database.[46] OMB attempted to eliminate many of the errors in FPDS by introducing a successor system—the Federal Procurement Data System-Next Generation (FPDS-NG), which began operation on October 1, 2003.[47] FPDS-NG was to "rely less on manual inputs and more on electronic 'machine-to-machine' approaches."[48] Despite the systems update, GAO said "[i]nformation in FPDS-NG can only be as reliable as the information agencies enter though their own systems."[49]

In September 29, 2009, testimony before the Senate Homeland Security and Governmental Affairs Subcommittee on Contracting Oversight, William T. Woods, GAO's director of Acquisition and Sourcing Management, said the following about FPDS information:

> Our past work has found that federal contracting data systems, particularly FPDS-NG, contain inaccurate data. FPDS-NG is the primary government contracting data system for obligation data. Despite its critical role, GAO and others have consistently reported on FPDS-NG data quality issues over a number of years.[50]

A 2012 GAO report reiterated its finding that DOD needs to "obtain better data on its contracted services to enable it to make more strategic workforce decisions and ensure that it maintains appropriate control of government operations."[51]

APPENDIX B. OBLIGATIONS TRENDS BY PSC CODE

According to FPDS-NG, product service codes (PSCs) are used "to describe the products, services, and research and development purchased by the government."[52] FPDS-NG breaks out contract obligations into 33 overarching PSCs; each of the nine product codes are represented by numbers

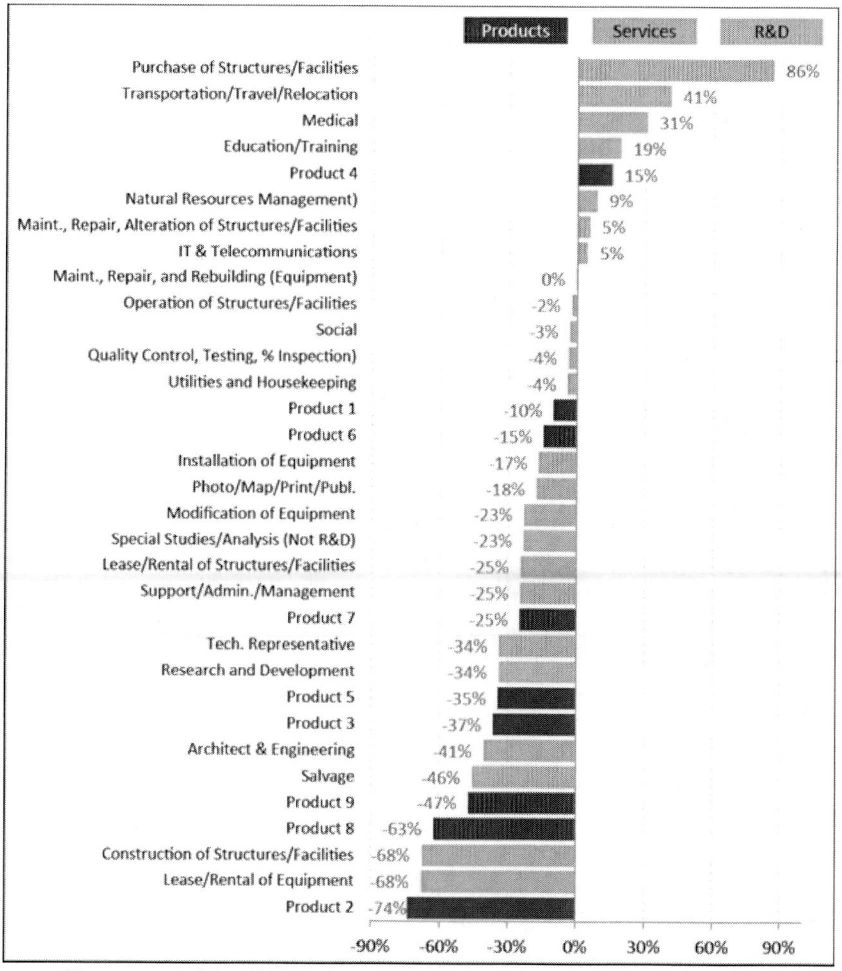

Source: Figure created by CRS.

Notes: Each two number code listed below corresponds to one of the 9 product codes represented in the figure. Codes beginning with a 1 are in the Product 1 category; codes beginning with a 2 are in the Product 2 category, etc.

Figure B-1 (Continued)

12 - Fire Control Equipment
13 - Ammunitions and Explosives
14 - Guided Missiles
15 - Aircraft and Airframe Structural Components
16 - Aircraft Components and Accessories
17 - Aircraft Launching/Landing/Ground Handling Equip.
18 - Space Vehicles
19 - Ships, Small Craft, Pontoons, and Floating Docks
20 - Ship and Marine Equipment
22 - Railway Equipment
23 - Ground Vehicles, Motor Vehicles, Trailers, Cycles
24 - Tractors
25 - Vehicular Equipment Components
26 - Tires and Tubes
28 - Engines, Turbines, and Components
29 - Engine Accessories
30 - Mechanical Power Transmission Equipment
31 - Bearings
32 - Woodworking Machinery and Equipment
34 - Metalworking Machinery
35 - Service and Trade Equipment
36 - Special Industry Machinery
37 - Agricultural Machinery and Equipment
38 - Construction, Mining, Excavating, Highway Maint.
39 - Materials Handling Equipment
40 - Rope, Cable, Chain, and Fittings
41 - Refrigeration, Air Conditioning Equip.
42 - Fire Fighting, Rescue, and Safety Equipment
43 - Pumps and Compressors
44 - Furnace/Steam Plant/Drying Equip, Nuclear Reactors
45 - Plumbing, Heating, and Sanitation Equipment
46 - Water Purification and Sewage Treatment Equipment
47 - Pipe, Tubing, Hose, Fittings
48 - Valves
49 - Maintenance and Repair Shop Equipment
51 - Hand Tools
52 - Measuring Tools
53 - Hardware and Abrasives
54 - Prefabricated Structures and Scaffolding
55 - Lumber, Millwork, Plywood, and Veneer
56 - Construction and Building Materials

58 - Communications, Detection and Coherent Radiation
59 - Electrical and Electronic Equipment Components
60 - Fiber Optics Materials and Components
61 - Electric Wire, and Power and Distribution Equipment
62 - Lighting Fixtures and Lamps
63 - Alarm, Signal, and Detection Systems
65 - Medical, Dental, and Veterinary Equipment
66 - Instruments and Laboratory Equipment
67 - Photographic Equipment
68 - Chemicals and Chemical Products
69 - Training Aids and Devices
70 - ADP Equipment Software, Supplies, Equipment
71 - Furniture
72 - Household/Commercial Furnishings and Appliances
73 - Food Preparation and Serving Equipment
74 - Office Machines
75 - Office Supplies and Devices
76 - Books, Maps, and Other Publications
77 - Musical Instruments
78 - Recreational and Athletic Equipment
79 - Cleaning Equipment and Supplies
80 - Brushes, Paints, Sealers, and Adhesives
81 - Containers, Packaging, and Packing Supplies
83 - Textiles/Leather/Furs/Apparel/Shoes/Tents/Flags
84 - Clothing, Individual Equipment, and Insignia
85 - Toiletries
87 - Agricultural Supplies
88 - Live Animals
89 - Subsistence (Food)
91 - Fuels, Lubricants, Oils, and Waxes
93 - Nonmetallic Fabricated Materials
94 - Nonmetallic Crude Materials
95 - Metal Bars, Sheets, and Shapes
96 - Ores, Minerals, and Their Primary Products
99 - Miscellaneous

Figure B-1. Change in DOD Contract Obligations by PSC Code. (FY2008-FY2014) (FY2015 Dollars)

from 1-9. Each of the service codes are represented by a single letter (R&D is represented by the letter "A"). Figure B-1 depicts changes in DOD contract obligations by PSC, from FY2008-FY2014.

Each of the 33 PSCs for services has a description identifying the types of contracts contained in the category; the nine PSCs for products do not have a description. Without a clear and logical system for categorizing products into overarching PSC categories—including descriptions for each category—breaking out such data is of limited value. To better understand what is contained in each product category, see the notes for Figure B-1.

APPENDIX C. TOP 12 COUNTRIES WHERE DOD OBLIGATES CONTRACTING DOLLARS

Table C-1. Top 12 Foreign Countries, by Place of Performance FY2015 dollars

Rank 2014	*Rank 2008*	Country	FY2014	FY2008	Unified Combatant Command
1	*2*	Afghanistan	$6,069,755,388	*$6,755,707,881*	CENTCOM
2	*10*	Japan	$2,028,067,694	*$969,497,409*	PACOM
3	*4*	Germany	$1,809,893,608	*$3,324,536,200*	EUCOM
4	*6*	South Korea	$1,770,236,660	*$1,675,148,579*	PACOM
5	*3*	Kuwait	$1,766,050,728	*$4,712,302,313*	CENTCOM
6	*8*	United Arab Emirates	$1,717,130,386	*$1,266,959,336*	CENTCOM
7	*17*	Saudi Arabia	$1,221,017,422	*$358,879,938*	CENTCOM
8	*40*	Bahamas	$767,756,656	*$61,548,573*	NORTHCOM
9	*54*	Kyrgyzstan	$668,580,013	*$19,885,188*	CENTCOM
10	*9*	Canada	$602,131,675	*$1,238,971,594*	NORTHCOM
11	*5*	United Kingdom	$552,568,786	*$2,072,609,195*	EUCOM
12	*13*	Switzerland	$340,954,545	*$727,402,503*	EUCOM
37	*1*	Iraq	$69,096,064	*$17,179,224,801*	CENTCOM

Source: Federal Procurement Data System—Next Generation, January, 2015.

End Notes

[1] CRS Report 98-721, Introduction to the Federal Budget Process, coordinated by Bill Heniff Jr., p. 2. The Government Accountability Office (GAO) defines an obligation as "a definite commitment that creates a legal liability of the government for the payment of goods and services ordered or received, or a legal duty on the part of the United States that could mature into a legal liability by virtue of actions on the part of the other party beyond the control of the United States. Payment may be made immediately or in the future. An agency incurs an obligation, for example, when it places an order, signs a contract, awards a grant, purchases a service, or takes other actions that require the government to make payments to the public or from one government account to another." U.S. Government Accountability Office, A Glossary of Terms Used in the Federal Budget Process, GAO-05-734SP, September 1, 2005.

[2] Federal Acquisition Regulation 4.602.

[3] U.S. General Services Administration, "FPDS-NG FAQ," at https://www.fpds.gov/wiki/index 2.php/FPDS-NG_FAQ.

[4] U.S. Government Accountability Office, Defense Contracting: Improved Policies and Tools Could Help Increase Competition on DOD's National Security Exception Procurements, GAO-12-263, January 2012, p. 11, at http://www.gao.gov/assets/590/587681.pdf. Based also on CRS review of data found in FPDS-NG.

[5] FPDS-NG lists the General Accounting Office, which in 2004 was renamed the Government Accountability Office.

[6] Office of Management and Budget, Budget of the U.S. Government, Fiscal Year 2016, Table S-1 Budget Totals, p. 91. Budget data based on outlays. Given the significant difference between outlays and obligations, this comparison is only intended to illustrate a rough magnitude of contract obligations within the context of overall federal government spending. Another method to quantify contracting as a percentage of government spending would be to compare contract obligations to the $3.614 trillion Total Obligations Incurred (offsetting collections and receipts) for all branches, as found in Office of Management and Budget, Fiscal Year 2016 Object Class Analysis: Budget of the U.S. Government, Fiscal Year 2016, Table 3-Bridge From Gross to Net Obligations, p. 83. This alternate method would not appreciably alter the results provided in this report.

[7] Deflators for converting into constant dollars derived from Office of the Under Secretary of Defense (Comptroller), Department of Defense, National Defense Budget Estimates for FY2015, "Department of Defense Deflators – TOA By Category 'Total Non-Pay,'" Table 5-5, p. 56-57, April 2014.

[8] Discussing the need to prioritize spending and make strategically informed decisions when cutting defense spending, Todd Harrison wrote:

CSBA has conducted a number of strategic choices exercises throughout the defense community challenging participants to develop a BCA-constrained strategy and defense program. Rather than simply cutting programs and forces to meet budget constraints, most teams have used the cuts as a forcing mechanism to rebalance DOD's portfolio of capabilities. While the strategies and associated priorities pursued by teams have differed, a common theme has been the need to make strategically informed investment and divestment decisions rather than just shrinking the size of the current force.

See Todd Harrison, Analysis of the FY 2015 Defense Budget, Center for Strategic and Budgetary Assessments, September 5, 2014, p. 30.

[9] For more information on the Budget Control Act, see CRS Report R43411, The Budget Control Act of 2011: Legislative Changes to the Law and Their Budgetary Effects, by Mindy R. Levit. Mindy Levit is no longer at the Congressional Research Service. For questions related to this report contact Steven Maguire at smaguire@crs.loc.gov or 7-7841.

[10] Robert Hale, "Sequestration: Don't Believe All the Hype," Breaking Defense, February 19, 2015.

[11] For a more detailed discussion of RDT&E spending, see CRS Report R43580, Federal Research and Development Funding: FY2015, coordinated by John F. Sargent Jr.

[12] RDT&E budget activities are broad categories reflecting different types of RDT&E efforts. The seven RDT&E budget activities are Basic Research, Applied Research, Advanced Technology Development, Advanced Component Development and Prototypes, System Development and Demonstration, RDT&E Management Support, and Operational System Development.

[13] Not all RDT&E categories have followed the same pattern. As Todd Harrison, analyst from the Center for Strategic and Budgetary Assessments wrote "Two areas of RDT&E funding have trended upward throughout the overall budget cycle: classified R&D and basic research. While both are cut slightly in FY 2015, they remain well above their pre-build-up levels." Todd Harrison, Analysis of the FY 2015 Defense Budget, Center for Strategic and Budgetary Assessments, 2014, pp. 24-25.

[14] Written Statement of Under Secretary of Defense Frank Kendall, U.S. Congress, House Committee on Armed Services, A Case for Reform: Improving DOD's Ability to Respond to the Pace of Technological Change, 114th Cong., 1st sess., January 28, 2015.

[15] Stew Magnuson, "DOD Official: Government Has Lost its Technological Edge Over Opponents," National Defense Magazine, January 27, 2015, p. http://www.nationaldefensemagazine.org/Pages/default.aspx.

[16] Based on discussion with CRS analyst, May 8, 2013.

[17] General Services Administration, Federal Procurement Data System-Next Generation (FPDS-NG) Data Element Dictionary, version 1.4, p. 98, February 15, 2011, at https://www.fpds.gov/downloads/Version_1.4_specs/FPDSNG_DataDictionary_V1.4.pdf.

[18] U.S. Government Accountability Office, Defense Acquisitions: Further Actions Needed to Improve Accountability for DOD's Inventory of Contracted Services, GAO-12-357, April 2012, Highlights, at http://www.gao.gov/assets/590/589951.pdf.

[19] NORTHCOM includes the United States, Mexico, Canada, and the Bahamas.

[20] CENTCOM includes Middle Eastern and central Asian countries, such as Egypt, Israel, Iraq, Afghanistan, Iran, Tajikistan, and Uzbekistan.

[21] U.S. territories in PACOM include American Samoa, Guam, Wake Island, and Johnson Atoll.

[22] SOUTHCOM includes South American countries.

[23] For purposes of this report, U.S. territories (including American Samoa, Guam, Northern Mariana Islands, Puerto Rico, the U.S. Virgin Islands, Johnston Atoll, and Wake) are deemed domestic spending. For a list of U.S. territories, see http://www.doi.gov/oia/islands/politicatypes.cfm.

[24] Based on Congressional Budget Office (CBO) methodology, the Iraqi theater includes Iraq, Bahrain, Jordan, Kuwait, Oman, Qatar, Saudi Arabia, Turkey, and the United Arab Emirates. See Congressional Budget Office, Contractors' Support of U.S. Operations in Iraq, August 2008, p. 3. For purposes of this analysis, the Afghan theater includes Afghanistan, Kazakhstan, Kyrgyzstan, Pakistan, Tajikistan, Turkmenistan, and Uzbekistan.

[25] In FY2009, the height of DOD spending during the conflicts in Iraq and Afghanistan, DOD had a base budget of $515.4 billion, more than 13 times the combined budgets of the Department of State, the U.S. Agency for International Development (USAID), and other foreign affairs agencies. In addition, DOD had a total workforce of more than 2.4 million, nearly 70 times the combined workforce of the Department of State and USAID. As a result of resource allocation, the Commission on Wartime Contracting in Iraq and Afghanistan stated that "Defense has become heavily engaged in stabilization and reconstruction—tasks seen as more akin to development than warfighting." See: Commission on Wartime Contracting in Iraq and Afghanistan, Transforming Wartime Contracting, Controlling costs, reducing risks, August 31, 2011, p. 132.

[26] Remarks delivered by Secretary of Defense Robert M. Gates at Manhattan, KS, November 26, 2007.

[27] FAR Subpart 4.602(2) and 4.602(4).

[28] U.S. General Accounting Office, Reliability of Federal Procurement Data, GAO-04-295R, December 30, 2003, p. 1, at http://www.gao.gov/assets/100/92399.pdf.

[29] Daniel I Gordon, Improving Federal Procurement Data Quality—Guidance for Annual Verification and Validation, Executive Office of the President, Office of Federal Procurement Policy, Washington, DC, May 31, 2011, at http://www.whitehouse.gov/sites/default/files/omb/procurement/memo/improving-data-quality-guidance-for-annual-verification-and-validation-may-2011.pdf.

[30] See U.S. Government Accountability Office, Improvement Needed to the Federal Procurement Data System-Next Generation, GAO-05-960R, September 27, 2005, at http://gao.gov/assets/100/93613.pdf; U.S. Government Accountability Office, Federal Contracting: Observations on the Government's Contracting Data Systems, GAO-09-1032T, September 29, 2009, at http://www.gao.gov/assets/130/123442.pdf; U.S. Government Accountability Office, Continued Management Attention Needed to Enhance Use and Review of DOD's Inventory of Contracted Services, GAO-13-491, May 23, 2013, at http://gao.gov/assets/660/654814.pdf.

[31] U.S. Government Accountability Office, Defense Acquisitions: Further Actions Needed to Improve Accountability for DOD's Inventory of Contracted Services, GAO-12-357, April 2012, Highlights, at http://www.gao.gov/assets/590/589951.pdf. See also, U.S. Government Accountability Office, Federal Contracting: Observations on the Government's Contracting Data Systems, GAO-09-1032T, September 29, 2009, p. Highlights. at http://gao.gov/assets/130/123442.pdf. In addition to this testimony, GAO has repeatedly made recommendations to improve FPDS data quality and reliability, including, for example, recommending that "OMB work with agencies to implement systems for contract writing that connect directly to FPDS-NG and provide confirmation of agencies' review and verification of the accuracy and completeness of their data in FPDS-NG." (U.S. Government Accountability Office, Data Transparency: Oversight Needed to Address Underreporting and Inconsistencies on Federal Award Website, GAO-14-476, June 2014, p. 9, at http://www.gao.gov/assets/670/664536.pdf.

[32] Office of Management and Budget, "Memorandum for Chief Acquisition Officers, Senior Procurement Executives, and Small Agency Council Members: Improving Acquisition Data Quality – FY 2008 FPDS Data," M-08-04, (Washington, D.C.: May 9, 2008); and Office of Management and Budget, Memorandum for Chief Acquisition Officers, Senior Procurement Executives, and Small Agency Council Members: Improving Federal Procurement Data Quality – Guidance for Annual Verification and Validation," at http://www.whitehouse.gov/sites/default/files/omb/procurement/memo/improving-data-quality-guidance-for-annualverification-and-validation-may-2011.pdf.

[33] U.S. Government Accountability Office, Defense Acquisitions: Further Actions Needed to Improve Accountability for DOD's Inventory of Contracted Services, GAO-12-357, April 2012, p. 2.

[34] For example, contract obligations performed in Texas were incorrectly coded as having taken place in Turkmenistan. Both Texas and Turkmenistan shared the same two letter code; the coding error occurred when TX was mistakenly entered into the country-code data field rather than the state-code data field, thus marking the place of performance as Turkmenistan. CRS found 32 instances where foreign locations shared the same two letter code as a U.S. state or territory; from FY2005 to FY2010, more than $1.4 billion in contract obligations listed as having been performed overseas were likely performed in the United States. This error was first identified in a news article published in Eurasianet.org. See Deirdre Tynan, "Turkmenistan: Memo to Pentagon – Austin and Ashgabat Are on Different Continents," EURASIANET.org, July 5, 2011, at http://www.eurasianet.org/node/63803.

See CRS Report R41820, Department of Defense Trends in Overseas Contract Obligations, by Moshe Schwartz and Wendy Ginsberg, July 22, 2011.

[35] CRS independently confirmed that data were adjusted.

[36] Information provided via e-mail to the authors on January 29, 2013. To implement the use of the three-digit ISO country code standard, GSA modified FPDS-NG to accept and return only ISO codes in the appropriate data elements and verified that the contractor charged with maintaining the system had the appropriate subscriptions with ISO to provide continuous country coding updates as they are released. The coding change document is available at https://www.fpds.gov/wiki/index.php/V1.4_SP_16.0.

[37] Information provided to the author by email from DOD on March 31, 2015.

[38] The data discrepancy appears only to occur when a user searches for data using the place of the contract's performance as a filter for responses. So, for example, the discrepancy would occur when a user employed the "standard report" to search for contracts that took place in Texas, and then ran the same search using the "ad hoc report."

[39] GSA's full email response read as follows: This apparent discrepancy is actually a feature of the data. Specifically, the difference that CRS is pointing out is due to the fact that IDVs are not required to have a place of performance, but can have obligated dollars against them. The Geographical Place of Performance Report requires a place of performance whereas the Federal Contract Dollars and Actions Report does not. The entire difference in the dollar amounts that CRS observed comes from dollars obligated against IDVs which do not have a Place of Performance.

Information provided from GSA to CRS via email on February 4, 2015.

[40] Based on CRS email exchanges and conversations with foreign-based investigative journalists and academics, April, 2015.

[41] P.L. 93-400, §6(d)(5).

[42] Ibid., §2. The section also states that Congress has a policy interest in "avoiding or eliminating unnecessary overlapping or duplication of procurement and related activities" and in "coordinating procurement policies and programs of the several departments and agencies."

[43] U.S. General Accounting Office, The Federal Procurement Data System—Making it Work Better, April 18, 1980, p. 3, http://archive.gao.gov/f0202/112171.pdf.

[44] Ibid., p. 4.

[45] Letter from Katherine V. Schinasi, Managing Director, Acquisition and Sourcing Management, Government Accountability Office, to The Honorable Joshua B. Bolten, Director, Office of Management and Budget, September 27, 2005, GAO-05-960R, p. 2, at http://www.gao.gov/new.items/d05960r.pdf.

[46] For example, in an October 1979 letter to former Representative Herbert E. Harris, II, then-Comptroller General Elmer B. Staats wrote of FPDS that "the extent of completion and accuracy varies for the different agencies involved." Moreover he wrote, "the Federal Procurement Data System relies on the integrity of many individuals to prepare the Individual Procurement Action reports ... and to prepare them correctly." Letter from Elmer B. Staats, Comptroller General of the United States, to The Honorable Herbert E. Harris, II, Chairman, Subcommittee on Human Resources of the Committee on Post Office and Civil Service, October 12, 1979, GAO/PSAD-79-109, pp. 1-2, at http://archive.gao.gov/d46t13/110552.pdf. In an August 19, 1994 report, GAO wrote "we found that the [Federal Procurement Data] Center does not have standards detailing the appropriate levels of accuracy and completeness of FPDS data.... [U]sers have identified instances where contractor names and dollar amounts were erroneous. We believe developing standards for FPDS data accuracy and completeness, then initiating a process to ensure that these

standards are met, would improve data accuracy and completeness." U.S. General Accounting Office, OMB and GSA: FPDS Improvements, GAO.AIMD-94-178R, August 19, 1994, p. 2, at http://archive.gao.gov/t2pbat2/152380.pdf. In a September 27, 2005, report, GAO wrote that "GSA has not informed users about the extent to which agencies' data are accurate and complete. This lack of confirmation perpetuates a lack of confidence in the system's ability to provide quality data." Letter from Katherine V. Schinasi, Managing Director, Acquisition and Sourcing Management, Government Accountability Office, to the Honorable Joshua B. Bolten, Director, Office of Management and Budget, September 27, 2005, GAO-05-960R, at http://www.gao.gov/new.items/d05960r.pdf.

[47] Letter from William T. Woods, Director, Acquisition and Sourcing Management, Government Accountability Office, to The Honorable Joshua B. Bolten, Director, the Office of Management and Budget, December 30, 2003, p. 3, at http://www.gao.gov/ new.items/ d04295r.pdf. FPDS-NG was designed and is maintained and updated by Global Computer Enterprises, Inc., through a contract with GSA.

[48] Ibid. According to GAO, most agencies were "expected to have computerized contract writing systems that [would] allow for direct submission of data to FPDS. Reliability of data [was] expected to improve because agency submissions to FPDS-NG [would] be based on data already in the contract writing systems, reducing or eliminate separate data entry requirements. The system provides for immediate data verification to detect errors. If errors are detected, agency procurement officials will have the opportunity to correct them immediately while the information is still readily available."

[49] Ibid.

[50] U.S. Government Accountability Office, Federal Contracting: Observations on the Government's Contracting Data Systems, GAO-09-1032T, September 29, 2009, p. 3, at http://www.gao.gov/new.items/d091032t.pdf.

[51] U.S. Government Accountability Office, Defense Acquisitions: Further Actions Needed to Improve Accountability for DOD's Inventory of Contracted Services, GAO-12-357, April 2012, Highlights, at http://www.gao.gov/assets/590/589951.pdf.

[52] For more information on PSC codes, see http://support.outreachsystems.com/ resources tables/pscs/.

In: Department of Defense Contract Obligations ISBN: 978-1-63483-768-2
Editor: Joseph Hodson © 2015 Nova Science Publishers, Inc.

Chapter 2

Department of Defense's Use of Contractors to Support Military Operations: Background, Analysis, and Issues for Congress*

Moshe Schwartz and Jennifer Church

Summary

Throughout its history, the Department of Defense (DOD) has relied on contractors to support a wide range of military operations. Operations over the last thirty years have highlighted the critical role that contractors play in supporting U.S. troops—both in terms of the number of contractors and the type of work being performed. Over the last decade in Iraq and Afghanistan, and before that, in the Balkans, contractors accounted for 50% or more of the total military force.

Regardless of whether future operations are similar to–or significantly different from– those of the past decade most analysts and defense officials believe that contractors will continue to play a central role in overseas military operations. Consequently, these observers believe that DOD should be prepared to effectively award and manage contracts at a moment's notice,

* This is an edited, reformatted and augmented version of Congressional Research Service, Publication No. R43074, dated May 17, 2013.

anywhere in the world, in unknown environments, and on a scale that may exceed the total contract obligations of any other federal agency.

Contractors provide a wide range of services, from transportation, construction, and base support, to intelligence analysis and private security. The benefits of using contractors include freeing up uniformed personnel to conduct combat operations; providing expertise in specialized fields, such as linguistics or weapon systems maintenance; and providing a surge capability, quickly delivering critical support capabilities tailored to specific military needs. Because contractors can be hired when a particular need arises and released when their services are no longer needed, contractors can be less expensive in the long run than maintaining a permanent in-house capability.

Just as the effective use of contractors can augment military capabilities, the ineffective use of contractors can prevent troops from receiving what they need, when they need it, and can lead to the wasteful spending of billions of dollars. Contractors can also compromise the credibility and effectiveness of the U.S. military and undermine operations, as many analysts believe have occurred in recent operations in Iraq and Afghanistan. Improved planning for and management of contractors may not eliminate all problems, but it could mitigate the risks of relying on contractors during overseas operations.

DOD's use of contractors has been a significant oversight issue for Congress in recent years. With the help of Congress, DOD has made substantial progress to improve its use of operational contract support; however, many observers believe the military is not yet sufficiently prepared to use contractors in future operations. In their view, better planning, expanded educating and training, ensuring sufficient resources to effectively manage and oversee contractors, and providing operational commanders with more reliable data can help build the foundation for the more effective use of contractors. In light of current and future budget constraints, some observers are concerned that DOD may not be able to sufficiently fund efforts underway to effectively prepare for the use of contractors in future operations.

DOD's extensive use of contractors poses several potential policy and oversight issues for Congress, including

1. To what extent will potential budget cuts or force structure changes impact DOD reliance on contractors?
2. To what extent is DOD preparing for the role of contractors in future military operations?
3. To what extent is the use of contractors being incorporated into DOD education, training, and exercises?

4. What steps is DOD taking to ensure that sufficient resources will be dedicated to create and maintain the capabilities to ensure effective operational contract support in the future?

Congress' decisions on these issues could substantially affect the extent to which DOD relies on contractors and is capable of planning for and overseeing contractors in future operations.

INTRODUCTION

Over the last two decades, contractors have played a critical role in U.S. military operations, making up more than half of Department of Defense's (DOD) total workforce in Iraq, Afghanistan, and the Balkans. With the end of combat operations in Iraq and the drawdown of forces in Afghanistan, DOD is turning its attention to preparing for future military operations. As reflected in recent defense strategic planning guidance, the United States must prepare for a diverse range of security challenges.[1] Although future contingency operations may differ from those of the past decade, many analysts and defense officials believe that contractors will continue to play a central role in military operations.[2] These observers believe that, in order to meet the challenges of future operations, DOD should be prepared to effectively award and manage contracts at a moment's notice, anywhere in the world, in unknown environments, and on a scale that may exceed the total contract obligations of any other federal agency.

This report provides background information and identifies issues for Congress on the use of contractors to support military operations. DOD's extensive use of contractors poses several potential policy and oversight issues for Congress and has been the focus of numerous hearings. Congress' decisions on these issues could substantially affect the extent to which DOD relies on contractors in and is capable of planning for and overseeing contractors in future operations.

THE ROLE OF CONTRACTORS IN MILITARY OPERATIONS

DOD has long relied on contractors to support overseas military operations. Post-Cold War defense budget reductions resulted in significant cuts to military logistics and other support capabilities, requiring DOD to hire contractors to "fill the gap."[3] Recent operations in Iraq and Afghanistan, and before that in the Balkans, have reflected this increased reliance on contractors supporting U.S. troops—both in terms of the number of contractors and the type of work being performed. According to DOD data, contractors, on average, represented just over half of the force in the Balkans, Afghanistan, and Iraq (see Figure 1).

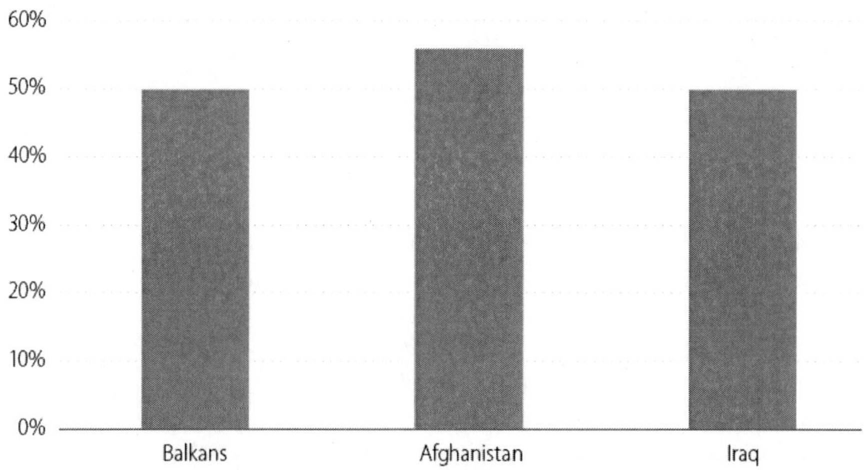

Source: Balkans: Congressional Budget Office. *Contractors' Support of U.S. Operations in Iraq.* August 2008. p. 13; Afghanistan: CRS analysis of DOD data, calculated as an average for the period September 2007–March 2013; Iraq: CRS analysis of DOD data, calculated as an average for the period September 2007–March 2011.

Note: DOD did not begin releasing data on contractors in U.S. Central Command until the second half of 2007.

Figure 1. Contractor Personnel as Percentage of DOD Workforce in Recent Operations.

As of March 2013, there were approximately 108,000 DOD contractor personnel in Afghanistan, representing 62% of the total force (see Appendix A). Of this total, there were nearly 18,000 private security contractors, compared to 65,700 U.S. troops.[4] Over the last six fiscal years, DOD obligations for contracts performed in the Iraq and Afghanistan areas of operation were approximately $160 billion and exceeded total contract obligations of any other U.S. federal agency (see Appendix B).[5]

What Is Operational Contract Support?

Operational contract support is the term used in DOD doctrine to describe the use of contractors to support military operations.[9] Operational contract support is the process of planning for and obtaining goods and services from commercial sources to support operations (including contractor management and oversight).

A number of different terms are commonly used by various observers to describe the use of contractors during operations, including *operational contract support, contingency contracting, expeditionary contracting*, and *wartime contracting*.

- *Contingency contracting* refers to the act of procuring goods and services in support of a contingency operation as defined in 10 USC 101(a)(13).
- *Expeditionary contracting* refers to the act of procuring goods and services in support of both overseas and domestic emergency operations.
- *Wartime contracting* generally refers to operational contract support in a wartime environment. This term was popularized by the establishment of the Commission on Wartime Contracting in Iraq and Afghanistan.[10]

Operational contract support encompasses, but is not limited to, all of these terms.

Operational contract support is more than just the process of executing a contract; it includes planning, identifying a requirement, contracting, management and oversight, payment, and contract closeout *(as depicted below).*

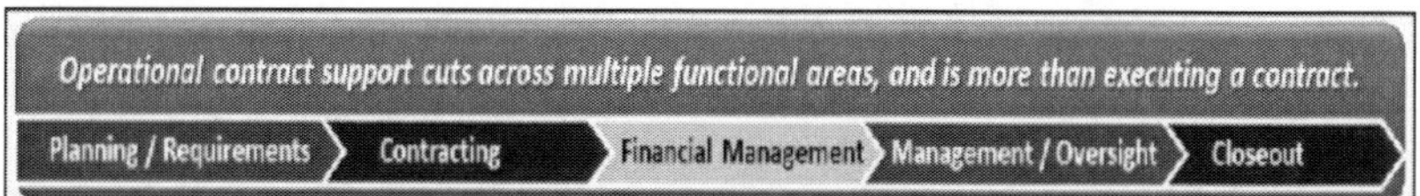

According to government officials and analysts, the military is unable to effectively execute many operations, particularly those that are large-scale and long-term in nature, without extensive operational contract support.[6] Even in short-term operations, contractors can play a variety of critical roles. For example, the first fragmentary order for *Operation Tomodachi*—DOD's response to the earthquake and tsunami that struck Japan in 2011—involved contract support.[7] Given the extensive role of contractors in military operations, many DOD officials and analysts consider contract management a mission-essential task.

DOD has recognized the role contractors are likely to play in future operations. As stated in its Budget Request for FY2013, operational contract support is a critical function in support of military operations, natural disasters, and unanticipated calamities.[8]

Contractors can provide significant operational benefits to DOD, including freeing up uniformed personnel to conduct combat operations; providing expertise in specialized fields, such as linguistics or weapon systems maintenance; and providing a surge capability, quickly delivering critical support capabilities tailored to specific military needs. Contractors are often responsible for such critical tasks as providing armed security to convoys and installations, providing life support to forward deployed warfighters, conducting intelligence analysis, and training local security forces. Because contractors can be hired when a particular need arises and released when their services are no longer needed, contractors can be less expensive in the long run than maintaining a permanent in-house capability. And when a decision is made to limit the number of troops on the ground, contractors can fulfill critical manpower needs.

Just as the effective use of contractors can augment military capabilities, the ineffective use of contractors can prevent troops from receiving what they need, when they need it, and can lead to the wasteful spending of billions of dollars—dollars that could have been used to fund other operational requirements.[11] Contractors can also compromise the credibility and effectiveness of the U.S. military and undermine operations, as many analysts believe happened in Iraq and Afghanistan.[12] Improved planning for and management of contractors may not eliminate all problems, but it could mitigate the risks of relying on contractors during overseas operations.[13]

DOD Was Inadequately Prepared for the Use of Contractors in Iraq and Afghanistan

DOD acknowledges that it was inadequately prepared to execute large-scale operational contract support in Iraq and Afghanistan.[14] Military commanders and service members have indicated that they were not prepared for the extent of contractor support in Iraq and did not receive enough training to prepare them to manage or work with contractors.[15] Some stated that they did not receive enough exposure to the role of contractors in military operations in the curriculum at professional military educational institutions.[16] An Army commission found that Contracting Officer's Representatives responsible for managing contractors are generally drawn from combat units and receive little, if any, training on how to work with contractors.[17] Many analysts and officials believe that the military did not have enough trained oversight personnel or an adequate infrastructure to effectively execute and manage contractors in Iraq and Afghanistan.[18] In January 2009, Secretary of Defense Robert Gates acknowledged DOD's failure to adequately prepare for the use of contractors when he testified that the use of contractors occurred

> without any supervision or without any coherent strategy on how we were going to do it and without conscious decisions about what we will allow contractors to do and what we won't allow contractors to do... We have not thought holistically or coherently about our use of contractors, particularly when it comes to combat environments or combat training.[19]

DOD acknowledges that there was no comprehensive plan for how to use contractors, and to what extent. As a result, the use of contractors was done on an ad-hoc basis, without significant consideration of implications for foreign policy and without putting in place the necessary oversight. Observers believe insufficient resources were dedicated to oversight, often resulting in poor performance, billions of dollars of waste, and failure to achieve mission goals. The Commission on Wartime Contracting found that, "too often using contractors [was] the default mechanism, driven by considerations other than whether they provide the best solution, and without consideration for the resources needed to manage them."[20]

Operational Versus Peacetime Contract Support

Contract support in operational environments is different, and often more complex, than contract support in peacetime. In peacetime, the goal of contracting is generally to obtain the good or service that is required.[21] The measurements of success are generally getting the right good or service, on schedule, and at a fair price.[22] During operations, however—and particularly in an expeditionary or counterinsurgency environment—cost, schedule, and performance are often secondary to the larger strategic goals of achieving military objectives or denying popular support for the insurgency. For example, in peacetime, the primary purpose of building a road is often to have the road built to specification in the most efficient and least expensive way. Other policy considerations may be factored in (such as small business or environmental concerns), but if the road is built on time, on schedule, and to the required specifications, the contract is usually deemed a success. During operations, however, these may not be the right measures, as other goals may be equally or more important.[23] In a counterinsurgency, winning the support of the local village is often more important than staying on schedule; in responding to a humanitarian crisis, rapidly providing critical supplies may be more important than an increase in cost or meeting some technical specifications.

Contract risks can also differ greatly between peacetime and operational environments. Peacetime risks generally include cost overruns, schedule slips, and poor performance. Additional risks must be considered when awarding a contract in an operational environment. As then-Commander, International Security Assistance Force, Afghanistan, General John Allen, stated in his contracting guidance to commanders in Afghanistan, it is important to

> look beyond cost, schedule, and performance. Evaluate the success of a contract by the degree to which it supports the Afghan people and economy and our campaign objectives. Include operational criteria in decisions to award contracts, such as the effect of the contract on security, local power dynamics, and the enemy.[24]

For these reasons, contract support in an operational environment is often far more complex to execute and difficult to evaluate than contract support in peacetime.[25]

The goods and services DOD buys during peacetime are very different from those during operations. In FY2012, 49% of all DOD contract obligations were for goods, 41% for services, and 10% for research and development (R&D).[26] By contrast, in Afghanistan, nearly 80% of DOD contract obligations in FY2012 were for services, 16% for goods, and 5% for R&D (See Figure 2).[27] Most analysts believe that buying services is more complex than buying goods, adding further complexity to using contractors to support operations.[28]

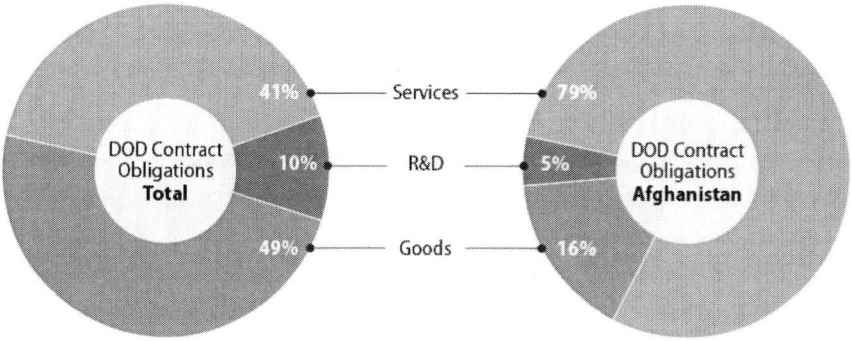

Source: CRS analysis of data from Federal Procurement Data System—Next Generation, March 2013.

Figure 2. DOD Peacetime vs. Operations Contract Obligation Trends, FY2012.

Some of the weaknesses of the current federal government acquisition process can be exacerbated by, and exploited in, an operational environment, making it more difficult to adhere to best practices. These weaknesses include inadequate acquisition planning, poorly written requirements, use of the wrong type of contract, and an insufficient number of qualified and capable acquisition and contract oversight personnel.[29] For example, in an expeditionary environment, it is more difficult to write a good contract that incorporates the sometimes competing goals of counterinsurgency contracting, more difficult to research and evaluate companies bidding on a contract, and more difficult to conduct oversight of projects being built in dangerous locations. It is also more difficult to protect against contracting fraud and corruption in countries that have weak law enforcement and judicial systems. Corrupt officials and warlords can exploit these weaknesses to divert contracting funds to their own coffers.[30]

Many of the differences between using contractors in peacetime versus in expeditionary operations were not readily apparent prior to military operations in Iraq and Afghanistan. One DOD analysis stated that standard acquisition funding procedures and regulations hindered effective execution of contract support in Iraq and Afghanistan. The report went on to state that, over time, virtually all leaders came to realize how different expeditionary operations are from business as usual in the United States.[31] Given the unique needs of DOD during an operation, peacetime contracting may not adequately prepare government personnel for the use of operational contract support. This has led many analysts and DOD officials to believe that the military needs to change the way it thinks about operational contract support, transforming it from an afterthought to a core competency.[32]

Consequences of Poor Use of Contractors in Iraq and Afghanistan

A number of analysts have attempted to quantify the extent of fraud, waste, and abuse in U.S. government contracts in Iraq and Afghanistan. The Special Inspector for Iraq Reconstruction estimated that waste associated with Iraq relief and reconstruction efforts totaled at least $8 billion.[33] The Commission on Wartime Contracting estimated that between $31 billion and $60 billion was lost to contract waste and fraud in contingency operations in Iraq and Afghanistan.[34] While the total cost of contract fraud, waste, and abuse may never be known, there is general agreement that the billions of dollars squandered by numerous federal agencies as a result of insufficient planning, management, and oversight could have been used to achieve other operational priorities.

Abuses committed by contractors, including contractors working for both DOD and U.S. civilian agencies, can also strengthen anti-American insurgents.[35] There have been published reports of local nationals being abused and mistreated by DOD contractors in such incidents as the summary shooting by a private security contractor of an Afghan who was handcuffed,[36] the shooting of Iraqi civilians,[37] and the abuse of prisoners at Abu Ghraib prison in Iraq.[38]

Insufficient contractor oversight can also undermine military operations. U.S. government investigations found that U.S. money for contracts in Afghanistan has been used to pay the Taliban in exchange for security. The Office of the Inspector General for the U.S. Agency for International Development found "indications that Afghan subcontractors... had paid insurgents for protection in remote and insecure areas of Afghanistan."[39] The majority report issued by the House Committee on Oversight and Government Reform's Subcommittee on National Security and Foreign Affairs similarly found evidence that U.S. contractors made protection payments to local warlords to secure safe passage of supply convoys. The investigation further found that protection payments may even have gone to the Taliban.[40] A Senate Armed Services Committee report found evidence of U.S.-funded prime contractors supporting the Taliban and subcontracting to warlords.[41]

According to many analysts, these events undermined the U.S. mission in Afghanistan and Iraq.[42]

Efforts to Improve Operational Contract Support

In light of experiences in Afghanistan and Iraq, and in response to legislation and the findings of numerous Government Accountability Office and Inspectors General studies, DOD has taken a number of steps to improve how it uses contractors during operations.[43]

DOD made significant organizational changes aimed at improving the current use of contractors, including establishing the Joint Theater Support Contracting Command; the Army Contracting Command (and its subordinate, the Expeditionary Contracting Command);[44] Task Force 2010;[45] the vendor vetting cell;[46] and the Joint Contingency Acquisition Support Office.[47] DOD also upgraded or expanded existing organizations, such as the Joint Staff's Operational Contract Support Services Division[48] and the U.S. Army Corps of Engineers Transatlantic Division.[49]

DOD established a Functional Capabilities Integration Board, co-chaired by the Deputy Assistant Secretary of Defense for Program Support and the Joint Staff Vice Director of Logistics. This board is a forum for senior leaders to come together to address critical operational contract support issues.[50] Many officials from across DOD and the Services have credited the Functional Capabilities Integration Board with improving coordination and implementation of operational contract support policies.[51]

DOD has also significantly expanded regulation, policy, and doctrine related to operational contract support, including the following examples:

- In 2009, DOD released a directive entitled, Orchestrating, Synchronizing, and Integrating Program Management of Contingency Acquisition Planning and its Operational Execution.[52]
- In 2010, DOD updated its Policy and Procedures for Determining Workforce Mix, which addressed contractor personnel as part of the total force.[53]
- In 2011, a major update to the Instruction Operational Contract Support was released, which established roles and responsibilities for managing operational contract support.[54]

- In 2012, DOD updated its joint planning and execution policy to include operational contract support in many non-logistical functional areas, such as intelligence, personnel, and engineering.[55]
- In 2013, DOD developed standards for using private security contractors.[56]
- DOD is updating its Joint doctrine, Operational Contract Support (originally issued in 2008), which is due for release in early 2014.[57]
- DOD has published various reference materials to assist deploying personnel.[58]

In addition, DOD is improving the business systems that support overseas operations. For example, in an effort to combat contract fraud, DOD took cash off of the battlefield by introducing an electronic payment system. According to a 2012 report, total in-theater cash payments to vendors in Afghanistan were down to 1% of all payments in FY 2012, compared to 39% in 2008.[59]

Since 2008, DOD has increased its total acquisition workforce by 21% to a total of over 150,000 acquisition personnel, which includes more than 30,000 contracting professionals.[60] DOD has also increased the number of Defense Contract Management Agency professionals supporting overseas missions.[61] To the extent that DOD improves its overall acquisition workforce, operational contract support may also improve.

What Has Enabled DOD Progress in Improving Operational Contract Support?

While acknowledging that much still needs to be done, many analysts and DOD officials generally agree that DOD has significantly improved operational contract support, with most of its progress occurring since 2010.[62] Understanding what enabled this progress could help DOD more effectively prepare for the use of contractors in the future.

The Experience of the Operational Force in Afghanistan and Iraq

As discussed above, military commanders and service members were not prepared for the extent of contractor support and did not receive enough training to prepare them to manage or work with contractors. However, their experiences on the ground quickly highlighted the critical role of contractors in military operations. These experiences, including the abuse of prisoners at Abu Ghraib prison in Iraq and the summary shooting by a private security contractor of an Afghan who was handcuffed,[63] led to numerous internal efforts to examine contractor support, such as the report of the *Commission on*

Army Acquisition and Program Management in Expeditionary Operations (known as the Gansler report). The experiences of the operational force also contributed to bringing the issue to the attention of senior leaders.

Senior Leadership Focus on the Importance of Operational Contract Support

Senior officials have made a concerted effort to elevate the importance of operational contract support and consider the role of contractors during contingency operations. In September 2010, then Commander, International Security Assistance Force, General David Petraeus, issued contracting guidance. The guidance articulated the importance of contracting in the overall mission, stating that contracting is "commander's business." The guidance also articulated clear and specific goals for contracting, including an emphasis on improving contract oversight and making contracting decisions that support overall mission objectives. In September 2011, within three months of assuming command, General John Allen updated the contracting guidance, with the intent of reinforcing the message that contracting plays a critical role in the overall mission.

In 2012, the Chairman of the Joint Chiefs of Staff stated, "we should acknowledge that [operational contract support] is no longer a niche capability.... Contractors are part of our total military forces."[64] This statement is consistent with those of other senior leaders, including the Secretary of Defense's 2011 memorandum on "Strategic and Operational Planning for Operational Contract Support (OCS) and Workforce Mix," which reinforced DOD-wide responsibilities for determining force mix, integrating contract support, as well as associated planning and resourcing.

Assigning Operational Contract Support Responsibilities to General Officers

Many analysts and DOD officials have stated that assigning general/flag officers to key positions has been critical to improving operational contract support.[65] This effort began in 2008, when the Army established five new general officer positions with responsibility for acquisition.[66] In 2009, Congress authorized five general/flag officer billets for acquisition.[67] In addition to these ten new positions, DOD appointed general/flag officers to key operational contract support-related positions, such as Task Force 2010, Task Force *Shafafiyat*, and the Afghanistan Operational Contract Support Drawdown Cell. Some of these officers came from the operational and logistics communities, helping to break down the barriers between contracting and operations.

Education, Training, & Exercises

DOD has expanded its training and exercises to address the role of contractors, and is continuing to incorporate operational contract support into Professional Military Education. In late 2012, DOD completed an Operational Contract Support Curriculum Guide, which captures specific learning objectives that will be used to inform Joint Professional Military Education at all levels.[68] In 2009, the Army launched a tactical-level Operational Contract Support course, which seeks to provide students a fundamental understanding of operational contract support planning, requirements development, and contract management. Over the last five years, over 1,500 DOD personnel have graduated from this course.[69] Based on the Army's training model, DOD is developing a *Joint Operational Contract Support Planning and Execution Course* for operational planners.[70]

In January 2013, the Army held its fourth annual Joint Contracting Readiness Exercise (JCRX), which was attended by over three hundred contracting professionals from the Army Contracting Command, to include Expeditionary Contracting Command, Mission and Installation Contracting Command, Contacting Support Brigades, and representatives from other Services.[71] According to officials, planning is underway for next year's exercise, to be held with U.S. Northern Command, making it the first such exercise conducted with a combatant command.[72]

Congressional Support

Many analysts and senior DOD officials have stated that without the efforts of Congress, DOD would not have been as successful at improving operational contract support. Examples of Congressional action that are often cited as having contributed to improving operational contract support include:

- legislation that led to establishment of the office of the Deputy Assistant Secretary of Defense (Program Support),[73]
- legislation establishing general/flag officer billets for acquisition,[74]
- legislation establishing the Defense Acquisition Workforce Development Fund, and[75]
- oversight hearings that raised awareness of contractor abuses and led to the creation of Task Force 2010.

In addition, the establishment of the Special Inspector General for Iraq, the Special Inspector General for Afghanistan, and the Commission on Wartime Contracting in Iraq and Afghanistan elevated the importance of the use of contractors and generated recommendations that were adopted by both DOD and Congress (see Appendix C for an expanded legislative history).

2006

- Directed DOD to develop joint policies for requirements definition, contingency program management, and contingency contracting.

2008

- Required contingency contracting training for non-acquisition personnel within DOD.
- Established the Defense Acquisition Workforce Development Fund.
- Required DOD, Department of State (DOS), and the U.S. Agency for International Development (USAID) to agree upon a central database for contract information.
- Directed DOD to develop regulations on the selection, training, equipping, and conduct of private security contractors.
- Authorized five Joint billets for General/Flag Officer to serve in Acquisition positions.
- Required DOD to establish policy to ensure proper development, assignment, and employment of military acquisition personnel.

2011

- Established a Government-wide contingency contracting corps to support domestic and overseas operations.
- Established oversight and accountability mechanisms for private security contractors in significant areas of military operations.
- Required DOD to review standards and certification of private security personnel.
- Required DOD to establish policy to ensure proper development, assignment, and employment of civilian acquisition personnel.

2012

- Amended the definition of a contingency operation.
- Required DOD to address contractor support in the Quadrennial Defense Review.
- Required DOD to amend the Defense Federal Acquisition Regulation Supplement (DFARS) to prohibit contracting with the enemy in the U.S. Central Command.
- Required DOD to amend the DFARS to allow access to the records of contractors and sub-contractors in U.S. Central Command.
- Granted authority for DOD to use 'reachback' contracting to support overseas contracting in Iraq and Afghanistan.

2013

- Extended expedited hiring authority to fill shortages in DOD's acquisition workforce through 2017.
- Required DOD to issue guidance on responsibility and authority for operational contract support policy, planning, and execution.
- Required DOD, DOS, and USAID to issue guidance regarding data collection on contract support for future overseas operations.
- Mandated the inclusion of operational contract support in certain requirements for DOD planning, joint professional military education, and management structure.
- Required Combatant Commanders to develop a contractor reliance risk assessment and risk mitigation strategy for operational or contingency plans.
- Described responsibilities of inspectors general during overseas contingency operations.
- Updated the responsibility of senior acquisition personnel within DOD, DOS, and USAID for contingency contracting and contract oversight.
- Required agencies to establish and maintain a database on price trends of items and services under Federal contracts.
- Required DOD, DOS, and USAID to have independent suspension and debarment officials.
- Stipulated uniform contract writing system requirements.
- Enhanced the responsibilities of the Chairman of the Joint Chiefs of Staff regarding the inclusion of operational contract support in National Military Strategy.

Source: CRS analysis of National Defense Authorization Acts for FY2007-FY2013.
Note: Dates represent year of enactment.

Figure 3. Select Legislative History.

Preparing for the Future

Despite the progress made to date, observers believe DOD still faces significant challenges in effectively utilizing and managing contractors to support current contractor support and prepare for future operations.[76] The 2010 Quadrennial Defense Review stated that the military's ability to effectively and efficiently use contractors to provide operational support "is an enduring priority and an area where continued improvements must be made."[77] Secretary of Defense Chuck Hagel reiterated this point when he stated

> I believe that investments made over the last few years... have vastly improved the Department's ability to effectively manage contractors on the battlefield. If confirmed, I will continue to improve our capabilities in this critical area.[78]

DOD officials in 2013 stated that it could take four to five more years to fully institutionalize operational contract support.[79] In light of future budget constraints, some observers are concerned that DOD may not sufficiently fund the efforts to effectively institutionalize operational contract support and prepare for the use of contractors in future operations. DOD officials, however, believe that modest funding of education, training, and exercises in the near-term will likely save billions of dollars, and enable greater likelihood of operational success in the future.[80] For example, the cost to hold the JCRX exercise is estimated to be less than $1.5 million annually.[81] Many analysts and senior DOD officials believe that Congress will play a pivotal role in determining the extent to which DOD funds and continues to implement its current initiatives.[82]

Cultural Change

A number of analysts have argued that one of the reasons DOD did a poor job planning for and managing contractors in Iraq and Afghanistan is that contracting was not valued within the culture of the military. Contractors were often an afterthought in planning and execution, frequently viewed by the operational force as someone else's problem and not as a warfighter's responsibility. Because contract oversight is often a lower priority, it was frequently assigned to people who did not have the necessary management skills or subject matter expertise. Many talented DOD officials did not consider acquisition a viable career path.[83]

According to the Commission on Wartime Contracting, GAO, Army reports, and others, such a transformation can only occur when there is widespread acceptance of the notion that that contractors are an integral part of the total force and that operational success may hinge on the ability to define requirements, efficiently allocate limited resources, and effectively manage tens of thousands of contractors.[84]

Many analysts suggest that changing the culture of the military is a prerequisite for creating lasting systemic change and improving operational contract support.[85] As discussed above, DOD has taken a number of steps to change its culture to appreciate the role of contractors in operations, including establishing operational contract support-related general/flag officer positions and expanding the education curriculum. Three common recommendations aim to continue to elevate the role of operational contract support within the culture of DOD:

1. Senior leadership must maintain its focus on articulating the importance of contract support in a sustained and consistent manner.[86]
2. The Professional Military Education curriculum must fully incorporate courses on operational contract support throughout its various efforts.[87]
3. Training exercises must be expanded and incorporate contractors playing the role that they would play on the battlefield.[88]

Observers believe these efforts will become increasingly important after the drawdown in Afghanistan, when the operational force no longer experiences firsthand the critical role of contract support.

Articulating the Importance of Contract Support

GAO and others have reported that the first step in improving contractor support at the strategic level is for senior leadership to consistently articulate its importance. Many analysts argue that without active and sustained support from senior leadership, the culture of the military is unlikely to change. According to these analysts, when management establishes priorities, articulates a vision, and aligns incentives and organizational structures to match these priorities, the foundation will be set for real change.[89]

As discussed above, senior leaders have increasingly articulated the importance of contract support. According to analysts and government officials, actions such as the contracting guidance issued by Generals Petraeus and Allen have raised awareness of the importance of contracting and the impact that contracting can have, both positive and negative, on operations. A number of military personnel believe that this contracting guidance represented a philosophical shift, requiring operational commanders to be more actively involved in contracting decisions and ensuring that contracting is more integrated with logistics, operations, intelligence, and strategy.[90]

A number of analysts argue that senior leadership must maintain focus on and continue to articulate the importance of operational contract support to ensure that cultural change is institutionalized and lasts beyond the current conflicts, beyond the tenure of current leadership. Further, given the new leadership in the Department of Defense, these analysts believe there is an increased need for senior leaders to reinforce the message that operational contract support is an enduring defense priority.[91]

Incorporating Operational Contract Support into Military Education

A number of analysts have argued that one key to reinforcing cultural change and improving operational contract support is better education.[92] They believe that increased education for non-acquisition personnel is critical to institutionalizing how the military approaches the use of contractors, both before and during overseas operations.[93] The Gansler report and numerous other officials and analysts argue that DOD needs to train warfighters, including operational commanders, on the central role contractors play in contingency operations and on their responsibilities in the process. These observers assert that operational contract support should be included in advanced officer courses, at command schools (e.g., senior service colleges and Sergeant Majors Academy), general/flag officer preparation courses, and in non-commissioned officer courses.[94]

While observers argue that failure to integrate contractor support into Professional Military Education can leave the military unprepared to manage contractors; GAO concluded that, "[T]he lack of contract training for commanders, senior personnel, and some contracting officers' representatives can adversely affect the effectiveness of the use of contractors in deployed locations. Without training, many commanders, senior military personnel, and contracting officers' representatives are not aware of their roles and responsibilities in dealing with contractors."[95]

While observers believe that DOD has made progress in developing and implementing courses on operational contract support,[96] some analysts contend these courses have not been sufficiently expanded and incorporated into the Professional Military Education curriculum.[97] A 2012 GAO report found that a number of commanders in Afghanistan reportedly did not always receive training on their contract management and oversight responsibilities.[98]

Including Contractors in Command Post and Field Exercises

A frequently stated guideline in the military is to 'train as you fight and fight as you train.' Given the extent to which contractors may be relied upon in future operations, conducting exercises without contractors could be akin to training without half of the force present. A number of analysts have called for incorporating contractors and contractor scenarios into appropriate military exercises to better prepare military planners and operational commanders for future operations.[99]

Despite increased inclusion of operational contract support in some exercises (such as Southern Command's PANAMAX 2012, Africa Command's Judicious Response 2012, and the Army's JCRX 2013), a number of reports have suggested that DOD has not sufficiently included contractor roles in battlefield exercises.[100] Some analysts have also argued that including contractors in field exercises could increase warfighter awareness of the presence of contractors on the battlefield and improve military-contractor coordination in actual operations.

Systemic Change

While changing the culture to embrace the importance of contract support may be an important step in improving operational contract support, many analysts argue that additional steps are needed: effective and efficient operational contract support, they argue, will not occur until an effective infrastructure is built to facilitate good contracting decisions. In 2011, the then-Senior Contracting Official-Afghanistan stated that a key to improving contracting is to identify the most glaring weaknesses in the acquisition process and build the infrastructure and support to overcome those weaknesses.[101]

Fundamental systemic weaknesses of contractor support that analysts frequently cite include

- poor or insufficient planning,
- lack of reliable data upon which to make strategic decisions, and
- lack of a sufficiently large and technically capable workforce to manage and oversee contractors and plan for their use.[102]

While acknowledging that building infrastructure capable of addressing these weaknesses requires significant, systemic change in the way DOD approaches and executes operational contract support, many analysts argue that without such systemic change, acquisition processes will not meet the needs of the military.[103]

Planning

Failure to include contractors in planning and strategy can put DOD at risk of being unable to get the capabilities it needs, when it needs them, and at an acceptable cost. For example, had DOD understood the extent to which it would rely on private security contractors in Afghanistan and Iraq, it might have put in place a more robust oversight and coordination mechanism earlier. In addition, a number of military bases in Iraq were not large enough to house contractors because DOD did not anticipate how many contractors would be deployed with the military. As a result, officials say DOD had to quickly find alternative housing for these contractors, which resulted in increased costs.[104]

Despite a requirement that contract support be integrated into the operational plans of certain combatant commands, GAO concluded that such integration does not always occur.[105] The Commission on Wartime Contracting found that "DOD has not adequately planned for using contractors for contingency support."[106] Some analysts have argued that a lack of planning is one of the reasons why DOD's current approach to managing service contracts tends to be reactive and not part of a well-conceived and planned strategic approach. Some DOD officials have indicated that more planners are still required to adequately include contracted support in future plans.[107]

Improving Data

Data reliability is generally considered to be a critical element in making informed policy decisions.[108] If data is lacking or is unreliable, there may not be an appropriate basis for measuring or assessing the effectiveness of contracting, making policy decisions, or providing transparency into government operations. In some circumstances, a lack of reliable data could lead analysts and decision makers to draw incorrect or misleading conclusions. The result could be policies that squander resources, waste taxpayer dollars, and/or threaten the success of the mission.[109]

DOD officials state that the International Security Assistance Force and the U.S. government have not accurately or sufficiently tracked data upon which to make strategic contracting decisions in Afghanistan.[110] Current databases are not sufficiently customized to track important contract data. Even when information is tracked, questions remain as to the reliability of the information. Given current concerns over the reliability of contracting data, the information in the central database may not be sufficiently reliable for decision making at the strategic level. This lack of data makes it difficult to determine to what extent the billions of dollars spent on reconstruction have contributed to achieving the mission.

DOD officials have acknowledged data shortcomings and have stated that they are working to improve the reliability and appropriateness of the data gathered. In a 2011 memorandum, General David Petraeus sought to establish and adequately support an Acquisition Accountability Office in Afghanistan to

- collect and manage data from all U.S. contracting and development agencies,
- furnish senior leadership, battlefield commanders, the U.S. Embassy, and the international community with information on what is being spent, with whom, and where, and
- build a more complete contracting operating picture.[111]

Looking beyond operations in Afghanistan, GAO concluded that data analysis from recent operations could help the development of a strategic plan to define contractor involvement in future operations.[112] Such data could help to more effectively determine future contractor support requirements. Putting in place data systems that can be used in future operations can provide commanders and policy makers with timely access to critical information to help them better gauge their needs, judge performance, and adapt to rapidly changing circumstances. Section 844 of the National Defense Authorization Act for Fiscal Year 2013 (P.L. 112-239) requires DOD, Department of State, and the U.S. Agency for International Development to issue guidance regarding data collection on contract support for future operations.

Dedicating Sufficient Resources to Managing Contractors

According to analysts and some government officials, there were simply not enough resources or personnel in theater to conduct adequate contractor oversight in Iraq and Afghanistan, leading to poor contract performance.[113] Insufficient resources or shortages in the numbers of oversight personnel can increase the risk of poor contract performance, which in turn can lead to waste, fraud, and abuse. DOD has documented how a lack of oversight has resulted in contracts not being performed to required specifications and to the theft of tens of millions of dollars' worth of equipment, repair parts, and supplies.[114] The Army Audit Agency reported in an audit of a particular contract that

> the inadequacies in contracting practices occurred primarily because... contracting offices didn't have enough personnel to conduct the needed contracting actions to ensure the Army received quality goods and services at the best attainable value.[115]

DOD has recognized the need to dedicate sufficient resources to provide effective oversight. According to the 2010 Quadrennial Defense Review, "to operate effectively, the acquisition system must be supported by an appropriately sized cadre of acquisition professionals with the right skills and training to successfully perform their jobs.... We will continue to significantly enhance training and retention programs in order to bolster the capability and size of the acquisition workforce."[116]

ISSUES FOR CONGRESS

The role contractors are expected to play in future operations raises a number of questions for Congress, including the following:

To what extent will potential budget cuts or force structure changes impact DOD reliance on contractors?

As discussed in this report, post-Cold War budget cuts resulted in an increased reliance on contractors. A number of analysts argue that DOD was over-reliant on contractors in Iraq and Afghanistan. Many analysts also argue that contractors were assigned responsibilities that should have been performed by government personnel. However, most analysts agree that DOD did not have the manpower to perform its mission without using contractors. A potential question for Congress is: To what extent will budget cuts, the imposition of personnel caps, or a restructuring of the force lead to an increased reliance on contractors?

To what extent is DOD preparing for the role of contractors in future military operations?

Planning can be critical to effective contractor management. DOD faces a number of challenges in planning for the use of contractors in future operations, including identifying the role contractors will play in future operations, anticipating the nature of future military operations, and accounting for possible budget cuts and changes to force structure. In light of these and other challenges, potential questions for Congress include: To what extent is DOD identifying the role of contractors in future operations? To what extent is the development of the future force structure being informed by a well-thought-out plan for how contractors will be used in future operations?

To what extent is DOD integrating the use of contractors into future operational planning? To what extent are lessons learned in contractor management and oversight being incorporated into doctrine and strategy?

To what extent is the use of contractors being incorporated into education, training, and exercises?

Observers believe education and training are critical elements in preparing for future operations. Richard Ginman, Director, Defense Procurement and Acquisition Policy, Department of Defense, recently testified before Congress that "the curriculum for each phase of joint and Service-specific Professional Military Education should include [Operational Contract Support] content appropriate for each phase of an officer's professional development."[117] Potential questions for Congress include: To what extent is DOD adapting what is taught in military educational institutions to address operational contract support? To what extent is DOD including contractor scenarios in post- and field-exercises? Are DOD efforts sufficient to prepare the operational force for how contractors will be used in future operations?

What steps is DOD taking to ensure that sufficient resources will be dedicated to create and maintain the capabilities to ensure effective operational contract support in the future?

Most analysts believe that effective use of contractors to support military operations requires dedicating sufficient resources to plan for, manage, and oversee the use of contractors. Yet many analysts have argued that insufficient resources are dedicated to operational contract support. This raises a number of potential questions for Congress: Does DOD have sufficient numbers of planners to effectively prepare for the integration of contractors into future operations? Does DOD have an appropriately sized and capable acquisition workforce? What steps are being taken to ensure that the infrastructure is in place to better track contractor data and measure contractor performance so that commanders and decisions makers will have necessary information upon which to make more informed decisions? Does DOD have the information technology capabilities necessary to support operational contract support planning and execution? In light of potential budget constraints, will DOD sufficiently fund efforts needed to institutionalize operational contract support and prepare for the use of contractors in future military operations?

APPENDIX A. NUMBER OF CONTRACTORS VS. NUMBER OF TROOPS IN IRAQ AND AFGHANISTAN

Table A-1. Contractor Personnel and Troop Level in Afghanistan September 2007–March 2013

	U.S. Nationals	Third Country Nationals	Local Nationals	Total Contractors	Troop Levels
Sep. 2007	3,387	2,864	23,222	29,473	24,500
Dec. 2007	5,153	3,815	27,552	36,520	24,600
Mar. 2008	4,220	4,678	43,438	52,336	28,800
Jun. 2008	4,724	4,121	32,387	41,232	34,000
Sep. 2008	5,405	4,381	58,466	68,252	33,500
Dec. 2008	5,960	5,232	60,563	71,755	32,500
Mar. 2009	9,378	7,043	51,776	68,197	52,300
Jun. 2009	10,036	11,806	51,126	72,968	55,107
Sep. 2009	9,322	16,349	78,430	104,101	63,950
Dec. 2009	10,016	16,551	80,725	107,292	69,000
Mar. 2010	16,081	17,512	78,499	112,092	79,100
Jun. 2010	19,103	14,984	73,392	107,479	93,800
Sep. 2010	20,874	15,503	34,222	70,599	96,600
Dec. 2010	19,381	21,579	46,523	87,483	96,900
Mar. 2011	20,413	23,537	46,389	90,339	99,800
Jun. 2011	23,294	25,666	44,158	93,118	98,900
Sep. 2011	23,190	27,912	50,687	101,789	98,200
Dec. 2011	25,287	34,811	53,393	113,491	94,100
Mar. 2012	34,765	37,898	44,564	117,227	88,200
Jun. 2012	30,568	35,118	48,050	113,736	85,600
Sep. 2012	31,814	39,480	38,270	109,564	76,500
Dec. 2012	33,444	35,714	41,246	110,404	65,800
Mar. 2013	33,107	34,375	40,314	107,796	65,700

Source: CENTCOM Quarterly Census Reports and "Boots on the Ground" monthly reports to Congress.

Notes: DOD did not begin releasing data on contractors in CENTCOM until the second half of 2007.

Table A-2. Contractor Personnel and Troop Level in Iraq September 2007–March 2012

	U.S. Nationals	Third Country Nationals	Local Nationals	Total Contractors	Troop Levels
Sep. 2007	26,869	45,422	82,534	154,825	169,000
Dec. 2007	31,325	56,368	75,898	163,591	165,700
Mar. 2008	29,351	57,270	62,757	149,378	160,500
Jun. 2008	26,611	62,650	70,167	159,428	153,300
Sep. 2008	28,045	72,109	63,292	163,446	146,800
Dec. 2008	39,262	70,875	37,913	148,050	148,500
Mar. 2009	36,061	60,244	36,305	132,610	141,300
Jun. 2009	31,541	56,125	32,040	119,706	134,571
Sep. 2009	29,944	53,780	30,007	113,731	130,000
Dec. 2009	27,843	51,990	20,202	100,035	114,300
Mar. 2010	24,719	53,549	17,193	95,461	95,900
Jun. 2010	22,761	46,148	10,712	79,621	88,320
Sep. 2010	20,981	42,457	10,668	74,106	48,410
Dec. 2010	19,943	40,776	10,423	71,142	47,305
Mar. 2011	18,393	36,523	9,337	64,253	45,660
Jun. 2011	18,900	34,974	8,815	62,689	46,010
Sep. 2011	16,054	29,213	7,370	52,637	44,755
Dec. 2011*	11,237	9,445	3,204	23,886	11,445
Mar. 2012*	3,260	5,539	2,168	10,967	-

Source: CENTCOM Quarterly Census Reports and "Boots on the Ground" monthly reports to Congress.

Notes: DOD did not begin releasing data on contractors in CENTCOM until the second half of 2007. The military mission in Iraq ended in December 2011.

*Includes DoD contractors supporting U.S. Mission Iraq and Office of Security Cooperation-Iraq.

Appendix B. DOD Contract Obligations

Table B-1. DOD Contract Obligations in Iraq and Afghanistan vs. Other Agencies' Total Contract Obligations FY2007–FY2012

	FY2007	FY2008	FY2009	FY2010	FY2011	FY2012	Totals
Department of Defense (Iraq and Afghan AORs)	$21,891,283,856	$28,875,512,402	$26,253,178,320	$27,625,427,448	$28,673,779,578	$26,254,357,426	$159,573,539,031
Department of Energy	23,157,132,401	24,768,818,050	31,664,208,980	25,691,143,398	25,064,910,632	25,119,296,953	155,464,510,413
Department of Health and Human Services	14,284,093,625	13,902,636,899	20,235,361,405	19,112,185,388	19,488,400,679	19,129,580,675	106,152,258,671
General Services Administration	13,144,929,701	13,369,927,514	15,602,222,549	15,602,222,549	12,606,959,366	8,639,612,490	78,965,874,169
Department of Veterans Affairs	12,684,246,066	14,890,683,047	14,805,695,906	16,242,524,319	17,632,877,962	17,132,179,960	93,388,207,260
National Aeronautics and Space Administration	13,127,897,278	15,067,086,283	15,299,616,912	16,089,328,286	15,400,490,866	15,143,707,272	90,128,126,896
Department of Homeland Security	12,470,642,016	14,031,586,352	14,289,230,571	13,581,990,656	14,217,244,691	12,412,476,555	81,003,170,841

Source: Federal Procurement Data System, as of June 2012 for FY2007; January 2013 for FY2012 data.

Table B-2. DOD Contract Obligations in Iraq and Afghanistan Theaters of Operation FY2007–FY2012

		FY2007	FY2008	FY2009	FY2010	FY2011	FY2012	Total
Iraq Theater	**Iraq**	$12,455,581,268	$15,177,699,901	$9,238,902,595	$7,039,364,738	$4,759,779,894	$667,118,490	$49,338,446,885
	Bahrain	496,937,727	1,124,980,986	1,913,165,418	544,732,445	479,778,452	313,731,235	4,873,326,263
	Kuwait	4,163,679,546	4,162,688,514	5,082,990,573	4,503,947,541	3,626,105,896	2,423,034,071	23,962,446,141
	Qatar	272,939,660	395,948,762	774,045,429	313,418,891	766,206,548	807,436,617	3,329,995,906
	Saudi Arabia	177,707,136	317,070,425	863,885,709	719,181,555	274,128,319	502,160,704	2,854,133,847
	Turkey	317,185,451	163,029,406	272,252,446	127,741,357	169,538,247	265,893,286	1,315,640,193
	UAE	220,509,874	1,119,332,017	251,296,568	2,374,103,632	1,024,349,143	1,491,473,321	6,481,064,556
	Oman	79,557,800	90,745,038	74,495,470	112,260,509	129,614,607	198,579,845	685,253,268.51
	Jordan	70,750,722	77,883,341	12,935,394	12,277,874	36,009,560	50,296,938	260,153,829.21
	Total Iraq Theater	18,254,849,182	22,629,378,390	18,483,969,601	15,747,028,541	11,265,510,666	6,719,724,506	93,100,460,887
Afghanistan Theater	**Afghanistan**	3,196,039,550	5,968,526,163	7,160,853,627	11,494,331,690	16,426,355,244	17,571,754,012	61,817,860,285
	Kazakhstan	5,113,688	26,038,365	41,970,867	59,116,526	68,631,726	72,909,975	273,781,146
	Kyrgyzstan	360,291,188	17,568,564	326,986,699	119,623,907	826,185,742	1,846,200,497	3,496,856,597
	Pakistan	62,848,359	203,365,810	221,731,297	160,078,547	59,342,433	16,068,851	723,435,298
	Tajikistan	-	11,000	951,307	3,384,903	3,233,262	8,241,038	15,821,510
	Turkmenistan	378,491	16,713,459	8,068,231	21,591,441	9,528,021	(2,664,251)	53,615,391
	Uzbekistan	11,763,398	13,910,651	8,646,691	20,271,894	14,992,485	22,122,798	91,707,916
Total Afghanistan Theater		3,636,434,674	6,246,134,012	7,769,208,719	11,878,398,907	17,408,268,912	19,534,632,920	66,473,078,144
Total Iraq and Afghanistan		**21,891,283,856**	**28,875,512,402**	**26,253,178,320**	**27,625,427,448**	**28,673,779,578**	**26,254,357,426**	**159,573,539,031**

Source: Federal Procurement Data System, as of June 2012 for FY2007; January 2013 for FY2012 data.

Appendix C. Select Legislative History

Concerned over DOD's use of contractors in Iraq and Afghanistan, Congress has held oversight hearings and enacted legislation aimed at improving operational contract support. This Appendix summarizes legislation affecting operational contract support in recent years.

National Defense Authorization Act for FY2007 (P.L. 109–364)

- Section 854 directed DOD to develop joint policies for requirements definition, contingency program management, and contingency contracting during combat operations and post-conflict operations.

National Defense Authorization Act for FY2008 (P.L. 110–181)

- Section 841 established the Commission on Wartime Contracting to investigate federal agency contracting for: the reconstruction of Iraq and Afghanistan; the logistical support of coalition forces operating in Iraq and Afghanistan; and the performance of security functions in such operations.[118]
- Section 1129 established the Special Inspector for Afghanistan Reconstruction to provide independent and objective: audits and investigations relating to programs and operations supported with U.S. reconstruction dollars; recommendations to promote economy, efficiency, and effectiveness; leadership on policies to prevent and detect waste, fraud, and abuse; and communication with the Secretary of State and the Secretary of Defense to keep them informed about problems and deficiencies relating to the reconstruction, the need for corrective actions, and progress on implementing corrective actions.[119]
- Section 842 directed the inspectors general with jurisdiction over the relevant contracts to conduct a series of audits to identify potential waste, fraud, abuse, or mismanagement in the performance of federal contracts for support to coalition forces in Iraq and Afghanistan, as well security and reconstruction efforts.[120]

- Section 861 directed DOD, the Department of State, and the U.S. Agency for International Development to enter into a memorandum of understanding regarding matters relating to contracts in Iraq or Afghanistan. The agencies subsequently entered into an agreement that designates DOD's Synchronized Predeployment and Operational Tracker (SPOT) as a common database for associated contract information.[121]
- Section 849 required contingency contracting training for non-acquisition DOD personnel.
- Section 851 required DOD to develop a strategic human capital plan for the acquisition workforce.
- Section 852 established the Defense Acquisition Workforce Development Fund for the recruitment, training, and retention of acquisition personnel.
- Section 862 directed DOD to prescribe regulations on the selection, training, equipping, and conduct of personnel performing private security functions under a covered contract in an area of combat operations.

National Defense Authorization Act for FY2009 (P.L. 110–417)

- Section 503 authorized five billets for Joint General Officer/Flag Officers to serve in acquisition positions.
- Section 834 required DOD to establish policy and guidance to ensure proper development, assignment, and employment of military personnel in the acquisition field.
- Section 870 established a government-wide contingency contracting corps to an emergency, major disaster, or contingency operation.

National Defense Authorization Act for FY2011 (P.L. 111–383)

- Section 873 required DOD to establish policies and issue guidance to ensure the proper development, assignment, and employment of civilian members of the acquisition workforce.
- Section 831 established oversight and accountability mechanisms for contactors performing private security functions in areas of combat operations.[122]

- Section 832 extended regulations on contractors performing private security functions to areas of other significant military operations.[123]
- Section 833 required DOD to review standards and certification for private security contractors.

National Defense Authorization Act for FY2012 (P.L. 112–81)

- Section 515 amended the definition of contingency operation.[124]
- Section 820 required DOD to address contractor support in the Quadrennial Review and other Defense planning documents.
- Section 841 directed DOD to amend the Defense Federal Acquisition Regulation Supplement to allow for the prohibition of contracting with the enemy in the United States Central Command theater of operations.
- Section 842. Directed DOD to amend the Defense Federal Acquisition Regulation Supplement to allow additional access to contractor and subcontractor records in the United States Central Command theater of operations.
- Section 843 authorized DOD to designate a single contracting authority that uses domestic 'reachback' capabilities in support of overseas contracting. This activity may use increased micro-purchase threshold and the overseas increased simplified acquisition threshold for contracts providing support to Operation Enduring Freedom and Operation Joint Dawn.
- Section 844 required an annual review of omnibus contracts providing support to contingency operations, to include the Logistics Civil Augmentation Program, be performed by a DOD competition advocate.

National Defense Authorization Act for FY2013 (P.L. 112–239)

- Section 846 required combatant commanders to develop a contractor reliance risk assessment and risk mitigation strategy for all operational or contingency plans.
- Section 861 required DOD (to include each military services and the Defense Logistics Agency), Department of State, and the U.S. Agency

for International Development to have an independent suspension and debarment official.

- Section 1273 assigned sustainability requirements for certain capital projects in connection with overseas contingency operations.
- Section 843 required DOD to develop and issue guidance on responsibility and authority for operational contract support policy, planning, and execution.
- Section 848 described responsibilities of inspectors general for overseas contingency operations.
- Section 849 updates the responsibility of the Chief Acquisition Personnel within DOD, Department of State, and U.S. Agency for International Development for oversight of contracts and contracting activities for overseas contingency.[125]
- Section 952 enhanced the responsibilities of the Chairman of the Joint Chiefs of Staff regarding the inclusion of operational contract support in national military strategy.
- Section 803 extended expedited hiring authority to fill shortages in the defense acquisition workforce through 2017.[126]
- Section 845 mandated the inclusion of operational contract support in certain requirements for Department of Defense planning, joint professional military education, and management structure.
- Section 844 required DOD, Department of State, and the U.S. Agency for International Development to issue guidance regarding data collection on contract support for future operations outside of the United States that involve combat.[127]
- Section 847 extended and modified reports on contracting in Iraq and Afghanistan through 2015.[128]
- Section 851 required agencies to establish and maintain a database on price trends of items and services under Federal contracts. 129
- Section 862 stipulated uniform contract writing system requirements.

End Notes

[1] Department of Defense, Sustaining U.S. Global Leadership: Priorities for 21st Century Defense, January 2012, p. 1, 4-7.

[2] Ibid. Strategic planning guidance states the U.S. must be prepared for a diverse range of security challenges; however, military "forces will no longer be sized to perform long-term, prolonged stability operations," p. 6. DOD's 2014 budget guidance further states that the military is transitioning from "a counterinsurgency-focused force to a force ready and

capable of operating across a full range of operations." See Department of Defense, Defense Budget Priorities and Choices—Fiscal Year 2014, April 2013, p. 8.

[3] Department of Defense, Report of the Quadrennial Defense Review, May 1997, Section 8. See http://www.dod.mil/pubs/qdr/sec8.html.

[4] Department of Defense, Contractor Support of U.S. Operations in the USCENTCOM Area of Responsibility to Include Iraq and Afghanistan, April 2013; Boots on Ground Report, March 2013.

[5] Iraq areas of operation are Iraq, Bahrain, Kuwait, Qatar, Saudi Arabia, Turkey, the United Arab Emirates, Oman, and Jordan. Afghanistan areas of operation are Afghanistan, Kazakhstan, Kyrgyzstan, Pakistan, Turkmenistan, Tajikistan, and Uzbekistan.

[6] Department of Defense, Office of the Undersecretary of Defense for Acquisition, Logistics, and Technology, Department of Defense Program for Contingency Contracting Planning, Oversight, and Visibility: Report to the Congress of the United States, November 2010, p. 18.

[7] Department of Defense, Pacific Command J4. Fragmentary Order for Joint Contracting Support Board for Operation Tomodachi. March 21, 2011, p.1-2. DOD directed US Forces Japan to establish a Joint Contracting Support Board within 24 hours. A fragmentary order is used to modify or execute a branch or sequel an existing operations order.

[8] Department of Defense, Fiscal Year 2013 Budget Request Overview, February 2012, p. 3-5.

[9] DOD's doctrinal definition of operational contract support is, "the process of planning for and obtaining supplies, services, and construction from commercial sources in support of joint operations along with the associated contractor management functions." See Joint Publication 4-10, Operational Contract Support, October 2008, p. 167.

[10] The Commission on Wartime Contracting was established pursuant to Public Law 110-181 to assess the extent of fraud, waste, and abuse associated with contracts supporting operations in Iraq and Afghanistan.

[11] Department of Defense, Quadrennial Defense Review Report, February 2010, p. 93. U.S. See also Government Accountability Office. Stabilizing And Rebuilding Iraq: Actions Needed to Address Inadequate Accountability over U.S. Efforts and Investments, GAO-08-568T. March 11, 2008, p. 4,6; Urgent Reform Required: Army Expeditionary Contracting, Op. Cit., p. 2-3.

[12] Many observers believe that the fallout from Abu Ghraib and other incidents, such as the shooting of Iraqi civilians by private security contractors hired by the United States government, have hurt the credibility of the U.S. military and undermined efforts in Iraq. See also: Department of Defense, Quadrennial Defense Review Report, February 2010, p. 93; Commission on Wartime Contracting In Iraq and Afghanistan, Transforming Wartime Contracting: Controlling Costs, Reducing Risk, Final Report to Congress, August, 2011, p. 5; U.S. Government Accountability Office, Operational Contract Support: Management and Oversight Improvements Needed in Afghanistan, GAO-12-290, March 29, 2012, p. 1-2.

[13] For example, according to an Army investigative report, a lack of good contractor surveillance at Abu Ghraib prison contributed to fostering a permissive environment in which prisoner abuses took place. See: Department of Defense. Investigation of Intelligence Activities At Abu Ghraib. August 23, 2004. p. 52. The report found "Proper oversight did not occur at Abu Ghraib due to a lack of training and inadequate contract management ... [T]his lack of monitoring was a contributing factor to the problems that were experienced with the performance of the contractors at Abu Ghraib." See also: Secretary of Defense Memorandum, Strategic and Operational Planning for Operational Contract Support and Workforce Mix, Jan 24, 2011, p. 1; U.S. Government Accountability Office, Operational

Contract Support: Sustained Leadership Needed to Better Prepare for Future Contingencies, GAO-12-1026T, September 2012, p. 1; Commission on Wartime Contracting In Iraq and Afghanistan, Transforming Wartime Contracting: Controlling Costs, Reducing Risk, Final Report to Congress, August, 2011, p. 28.

[14] U.S. Congress, House Committee on Armed Services, Hearing on Operational Contract Support: Learning from the Past and Preparing for the Future, Joint Testimony of Hon. Alan F. Estevez, Assistant Secretary of Defense, Logistics and Materiel Readiness, and Brigadier General Craig C. Crenshaw, Vice Director, Joint Staff, J-4, 112th Congress, September 12, 2012, p. 2; U.S. Army, Army Operational Contract Support Audit Analysis Project, Results Summary, April 29, 2011, p. 1.

[15] U.S. Government Accountability Office, DOD Needs to Reexamine Its Extensive Reliance on Contractors and Continue to Improve Management and Oversight, GAO-08-572T, Highlights page, March 11, 2008; also based on discussions with military personnel deployed in Iraq.

[16] U.S. Government Accountability Office, Operational Contract Support: Management and Oversight Improvements Needed in Afghanistan, GAO-12-290, March 2012, p. 17; based on numerous CRS discussions with DOD personnel from 2009-2013.

[17] Urgent Reform Required: Army Expeditionary Contracting, Op. Cit., p. 43.

[18] U.S. Government Accountability Office, Afghanistan: Key Oversight Issues, GAO-13-218SP, February 2013, p. 31; Operational Contract Support: Management and Oversight Improvements Needed in Afghanistan, Op. Cit, p. 9, 23, 25; U.S. Congress, Senate Committee on Homeland Security and Governmental Affairs, Ad Hoc Subcommittee on Contracting Oversight, The Comprehensive Contingency Contracting Reform Act of 2012 (S.2139), Testimony of Richard Ginman, Director, Defense Procurement and Acquisition Policy, Department of Defense, 112th Cong., 2nd sess., April 17, 2012, p. 6; Kathryn T.H. Syzmanski, Command Counsel U.S. Army Materiel Command in Atlanta on August 9, 2004. American Bar Association Section of Public Contract Law, Contractors on the Battlefield: Exploration of Unique Liability and Human Relations Issues, Volume II. See also CRS Report R42084, Wartime Contracting in Afghanistan: Analysis and Issues for Congress, by Moshe Schwartz; U.S. Government Accountability Office, Military Operations: High-Level DOD Action Needed to Address Long-standing Problems with Management and Oversight of Contractors Supporting Deployed Forces, GAO-07-145, December 18, 2006.

[19] U.S. Congress, Senate Committee on Armed Services, To Receive Testimony on the Challenges Facing the Department of Defense, 110th Cong., 2nd sess., January 27, 2009.

[20] Commission on Wartime Contracting in Iraq and Afghanistan, At What Risk? Correcting Over-reliance on Contractors in Contingency Operations, Second Interim Report to Congress, February 24, 2011, Forward.

[21] Additional factors can come in to play in peacetime, including stimulating the economy and creating jobs.

[22] The Federal Acquisition Regulation (FAR 1.102) states that the goal of the government acquisition system is to promote public policy considerations, such as transparency, competition, and promotion of small business. Even within this context, these considerations often play a secondary role to the general focus on cost, schedule and performance.

[23] A number of analysts have raised concerns over the sustainability of infrastructure projects in Afghanistan. According to the Commission on Wartime Contracting in Iraq and Afghanistan, "spotting and assessing the threat of waste from an unsustainable project is not

as simple as examining construction quality, performance, of services, schedule, compliance, or the accuracy of labor and materiel billings." See Commission on Wartime Contracting in Iraq and Afghanistan, Sustainability: Hidden Costs Risk New Waste, June 3, 2011, p. 2.

[24] General John R. Allen, Commander International Security Assistance Force-Afghanistan, COMISAF's Counterinsurgency (COIN) Contracting Guidance, Headquarters, International Security Assistance Force-Afghanistan, Kabul, Afghanistan, September 18, 2011, p. 3.

[25] For an in-depth discussion of the differences between operational and peacetime contracting, see CRS Report R42084, Wartime Contracting in Afghanistan: Analysis and Issues for Congress, by Moshe Schwartz.

[26] Calculations are based on DOD total contract obligations in FY2012 from Federal Procurement Data System—Next Generation, March, 2013. For further analysis of contract obligations, see CRS Report R41820, Department of Defense Trends in Overseas Contract Obligations, by Moshe Schwartz and Wendy Ginsberg.

[27] Calculations are based on DOD contract obligations for performance in Afghanistan in FY2012 from Federal Procurement Data System—Next Generation, March, 2013. Values do not add up to 100% due to rounding.

[28] Office of the Undersecretary of Defense (AT&L), Improvements to Services Contracting, Report of the Defense Science Board Task Force, March 2011, Executive Summary.

[29] See U.S. Government Accountability Office, High Risk Series, An Update, GAO-11-278, February, 2011, p. 125, and U.S. Government Accountability Office, High Risk Series, An Update, GAO-13-283, February 2013, p. 213.

[30] See CRS Report R42084, Wartime Contracting in Afghanistan: Analysis and Issues for Congress, by Moshe Schwartz.

[31] United States Corps of Engineers, Core Counterinsurgency Asset: Lessons from Iraq and Afghanistan for United States Army Corps of Engineers, May 2012, p. xv.

[32] Commission on Wartime Contracting In Iraq and Afghanistan, At What Risk? Correcting Over-reliance on Contractors in Contingency Operations, Second Interim Report to Congress, February 24, 2011, p. 2.

[33] Special Inspector for Iraq Reconstruction, Learning from Iraq: A Final Report from the Special Inspector for Iraq Reconstruction, March 2013, p. 20. $8 billion estimate only includes projects associated with the five major funding streams associated with relief and reconstruction.

[34] Commission on Wartime Contracting In Iraq and Afghanistan, Transforming Wartime Contracting: Controlling Costs, Reducing Risk, Final Report to Congress, August, 2011, p. 1.

[35] Chairman of the Joint Chiefs of Staff, Operational Contract Support, Joint Publication 4-10, October 17, 2008, pp. IV-20; See also Counterinsurgency, p. 1-9. Operational Contract Support recognizes that local nationals may not always draw a distinction between government contractors and the U.S. military.

[36] Bruce Alpert, "Killing in Afghanistan hits very close to home; N.O. man is accused of cold-blooded crime," Times-Picayune, December 17, 2008, p. 1.

[37] Mark Townsend, "National: Iraq victims sue UK security firm: Guards employed by Hampshire-based company are," The Observer, January 11, 2009, p. 14.

[38] Department of Defense, Investigation of Intelligence Activities at Abu Ghraib, August 23, 2004. See http://oai.dtic.mil/oai/oai?verb=getRecord&metadataPrefix=html& identifier= ADA429125. The contractors involved in the Abu Ghraib incident are generally considered not to have been private security contractors.

[39] Office of the Inspector General for the U.S. Agency for International Development , Report Review of Security Costs Charged to USAID Projects in Afghanistan, Review Report No. 5-306-10-002-S, September 29, 2010, p. 2.

[40] Subcommittee on National Security and Foreign Affairs of the House Committee on Oversight and Government Reform, "Warlord Inc.: Extortion and Corruption Along the U.S. Supply Chain in Afghanistan," June 22, 2010.

[41] Senate Armed Services Committee, "Inquiry into the Role and Oversight of Private Security Contractors in Afghanistan," October 7, 2010.

[42] Commission on Wartime Contracting In Iraq and Afghanistan, Transforming Wartime Contracting: Controlling Costs, Reducing Risk, Final Report to Congress, August, 2011, p. 74; U.S. Government Accountability Office, Afghanistan: Key Oversight Issues, GAO-13-218SP, February 2013, p. 27.

[43] U.S. Government Accountability Office, Warfighter Support: DOD Needs Additional Steps to Fully Integrate Operational Contract Support into Contingency Planning, GAO-13-212, February 8, 2013, p. 3.

[44] The Army Contracting Command, established in 2008, is a two-star level command responsible for performing the majority of the U.S. Army's contracting activities around the world. See: http://www.acc.army.mil/about/.

[45] DOD established Task Force 2010 in July 2010 to help commanders and acquisition personnel better understand with whom they are doing business, to conduct investigations to gain visibility into the flow of money at the subcontractor levels, and to promote and distribute best contracting practices. See CRS Report R42084, Wartime Contracting in Afghanistan: Analysis and Issues for Congress, by Moshe Schwartz.

[46] The Afghanistan Vendor Vetting Cell was established to ensure that government contracts are not awarded to companies with ties to insurgents, warlords, or criminal networks. The cell was set up in the fall of 2010 and is based in Central Command headquarters in Tampa, FL. See CRS Report R42084, Wartime Contracting in Afghanistan: Analysis and Issues for Congress, by Moshe Schwartz.

[47] DOD established the Joint Contingency Acquisition Support Office (JCASO) to provide the joint force commander with the necessary assistance to plan, support, and oversee contingency contracting activities during the initial phases of a contingency operation. According to DOD, seventeen (17) JCASO planners are allocated among the Geographic Combatant Commands to assist the commander in identifying gaps where contractor support capability may be required. See: Department of Defense, Contractor Support of U.S. Operations in the USCENTCOM Area of Responsibility to Include Iraq and Afghanistan, January 2013.

[48] The Joint Staff J4's Logistics Service Division became the Operational Contract Support Services Division in 2010. This Division provides plans, policy, guidance, and oversight on operational contract support matters for the Chairman of the Joint Chiefs of Staff in accordance with Title 10 USC Section 153.

[49] The U.S. Army Corps of Engineers activated the Transatlantic Division in 2009 to consolidate requirements and manage its engineering operations throughout the Middle East and Central Asia.

[50] The Operational Contract Support Functional Capabilities Integration Board was chartered based on the authority set forth in Section 854 of the John Warner National Defense Authorization Act for 2007 (Public Law 109-364). See http://www.acq.osd.mil/log/PS /fcib.html.

[51] Based on CRS interviews with DOD officials, February 2013. The Functional Capabilities Integration Board is overseeing the implementation of an Operational Contract Support Action Plan, which serves to track DOD's progress in closing the ten highest-priority operational contract support capability gaps. According to officials, the plan will guide planning and programing efforts to close urgent gaps by 2016.

[52] DOD Directive 3020.49 Orchestrating, Synchronizing, and Integrating Program Management of Contingency Acquisition Planning and its Operational Execution, March 2009.

[53] DOD Instruction 1100.22, Policy and Procedures for Determining Workforce Mix, April 2010. DOD is in the process of updating DOD Instruction 1100.22 as well as DOD Directive 1100.4, Guidance for Manpower Management.

[54] DOD Instruction 3020.41, Operational Contract Support, December 2011. In 2012, this Instruction was codified in 32 Code of Federal Regulations Part 158.

[55] Chairman of the Joint Chiefs of Staff Manual 3130.03, Adaptive Planning and Execution (APEX) Planning Formats and Guidance, October 2012.

[56] Private Security Contractor standards were required by Section 833 of the NDAA for FY2011. The American National Standards Institute validated these standards in March 2013.

[57] Joint Publication 4-10, Operational Contract Support, October 2008. Based on CRS discussion with DOD officials on February 6, 2013.

[58] DOD released its 4th Edition of the Defense Contingency Contracting Handbook and Deployed Contracting Officer's Representative Handbook in September 2012. See http://www.acq.osd.mil/dpap/pacc/cc/index.html.

[59] Department of Defense, Fiscal Year 2013 Budget Request Overview, February 2012, p. 3-7.

[60] Department of Defense, Defense Acquisition Workforce Annual Count Comparison FY 2001-FY 2012, PowerPoint Presentation, February 2013, p. 2-3.

[61] The Defense Contract Management Agency provides contract administration services to the Department of Defense, including contract management, quality assurance, and property administration. See Defense Contract Management Agency, State of the Agency: Fiscal Year 2012, p. 3-4, 11.

[62] Based on CRS discussions with DOD officials and analysis of contractor support from 2008-2013; see also U.S. Government Accountability Office, Warfighter Support: DOD Needs Additional Steps to Fully Integrate Operational Contract Support into Contingency Planning, GAO-13-212, February 8, 2013, p. 31.

[63] Bruce Alpert, "Killing in Afghanistan hits very close to home; N.O. man is accused of cold-blooded crime," Times- Picayune, December 17, 2008, p. 1.

[64] General Martin Dempsey, Chairman of the Joint Chiefs of Staff, Opening Remarks to Operational Contract Support Leader's Conference, March 6, 2012.

[65] In its final report, the Gansler Commission stated that establishing General Officer positions responsible for contracting would, "improve support to military operations by having officers at the table planning and supporting the operation" and "increase the attractiveness of the contracting corps as a profession to quality officers," p. 5.

[66] The Army established five General Officer billets for acquisition in 2009 based on recommendations made by the Gansler Commission. According to DOD, these positions currently reside within the: Army Contracting Command; Expeditionary Contracting Command; Mission and Installation Contracting Command; U.S. Army Corps of Engineers National Contracting Organization; and the office of the Assistant Secretary of the Army for Acquisition, Logistics, and Technology, in the office of the Deputy Assistant Secretary of the Army for Procurement. See: Assistant Secretary of Defense for Logistics and Materiel Readiness, Cost Consciousness in Contingency Contracting, June 2012, p. 4.

[67] Congress authorized five Joint billets for acquisition General/Flag Officers in Section 503 of the National Defense Authorization Act for 2009 (P. L. 110-147). According to DOD, these billets are assigned to the: Defense Contract Management Agency; Joint Contingency Acquisition Support Office; U.S. Central Command's Joint Theater Support Contracting Command; and the Under Secretary of Defense for Acquisition, Technology and Logistics, Office of Defense Procurement and Acquisition Policy. See: Assistant Secretary of Defense for Logistics and Materiel Readiness, Cost Consciousness in Contingency Contracting, June 2012, p. 4.

[68] Operational Contract Support has been on the Chairman of the Joint Chiefs of Staff's list of Special Areas of Emphasis for Professional Military Education since 2009. See Operational Contract Support Learning Framework at http://www.acq.osd.mil/log/PS/OCS_edu.html.

[69] Based on CRS discussion with Army officials on April 11, 2013.

[70] U.S. Congress, House Committee on Armed Services, Hearing on Operational Contract Support: Learning from the Past and Preparing for the Future, Joint Testimony of Hon. Alan F. Estevez, Assistant Secretary of Defense, Logistics and Materiel Readiness, and Brigadier General Craig C. Crenshaw, Vice Director, Joint Staff, J-4, 112th Congress, September 12, 2012, p. 9.

[71] U.S. Army Contracting Command, Joint Contracting Readiness Exercise 2013 Information Brief, PowerPoint Presentation, April 2013, slide 13.

[72] Ibid., slide 14.

[73] Section 854 of the National Defense Authorization Act for 2007 (P.L. 109-364) led to the establishment of an Assistant Deputy Undersecretary of Defense for Program Support, which DOD later elevated to the Deputy Assistant Secretary of Defense for Program Support.

[74] Section 503 of the National Defense Authorization Act for 2009 (P.L. 110-147) added five Joint billets for General/Flag Officers to serve in Acquisition positions.

[75] Section 852 of the National Defense Authorization Act for 2008 (P.L. 110-181) enacted the Defense Acquisition Workforce Development Fund for the recruitment, training, and retention of acquisition personnel.

[76] U.S. Government Accountability Office, Warfighter Support: DOD Needs Additional Steps to Fully Integrate Operational Contract Support into Contingency Planning, GAO-13-212, February 8, 2013, p. 31; Commission on Wartime Contracting In Iraq and Afghanistan, Transforming Wartime Contracting: Controlling Costs, Reducing Risk, Final Report to Congress, August, 2011, p. 19; U.S. Government Accountability Office, Operational Contract Support: Management and Oversight Improvements Needed in Afghanistan, GAO-12-290, March 29, 2012, p. Highlights; U.S. Congress, Senate Committee on Homeland Security and Governmental Affairs, Ad Hoc Subcommittee on Contracting Oversight, The Comprehensive Contingency Contracting Reform Act of 2012 (S.2139), Statement for the Record of Katherine Schinasi, 112th Cong., 2nd sess., April 17, 2012, p. 1; Joint Chiefs of Staff, J-4 (Logistics), Operational Contract Support Strategic Update, June 2012.

[77] Department of Defense, Quadrennial Defense Review Report, February 2010, p. 76.

[78] U.S. Congress, Senate, Written Response to Advance Policy Questions for the Honorable Chuck Hagel, Nominee to be Secretary of Defense, 113th Cong., January 2013, p. 101.

[79] Joint Staff J4, "Operational Contract Support Strategic Update," 6th Annual Joint Staff Leader's Conference, March 5, 2013, p. 6.

[80] Based on CRS discussions with DOD officials, February-April, 2013. The importance of investing sufficient resources to ensure that the workforce is capable of managing the

acquisition process was reinforced in Secretary Hagel's written confirmation testimony response to the Senate Armed Services Committee. The response reads

[Question] Do you agree that the Department would be "penny-wise and pound foolish" to try to save money by cutting corners on its acquisition workforce at the risk or losing control over the hundreds of billions of dollars that it spends every year on the acquisition of products and services?

[Answer] Yes. It is imperative that the Department of Defense act as a good steward of the resources entrusted to it by the American people. A properly qualified and sized acquisition workforce is central to maintaining this stewardship....

[81] Based on data provided by Army officials, March, 2013. According to officials, Defense Acquisition Workforce Development funds were used to fund JCRX 2013.

[82] Based on CRS discussions with analysts and DOD officials, February-April, 2013.

[83] Commission on Wartime Contracting In Iraq and Afghanistan, Transforming Wartime Contracting: Controlling Costs, Reducing Risk, Final Report to Congress, August, 2011, p. 117; Office of the Undersecretary of Defense (AT&L), Improvements to Services Contracting, Report of the Defense Science Board Task Force, March 2011, p. 23.

[84] See Urgent Reform Required: Army Expeditionary Contracting, p. 9, which states, "the Army apparently has not valued the skill and experience required to perform those processes.... [W]ithout significant systemic change, the Army acquisition processes [contracting process] can be expected to inevitably return to below-mediocrity." See also New American Foundation, Changing the Culture of Pentagon Contracting, November 5, 2008.

[85] U.S. Government Accountability Office, Contingency Contracting: Observations on Actions Needed to Address Systemic Challenges, GAO-11-580, April 25, 2011, p. 9; Defense Business Board, Task Group on A Culture of Savings, Implementing Behavioral Change in DOD, January, 2011, p. 2-3.

[86] U.S. Government Accountability Office, Operational Contract Support: Sustained Leadership Needed to Better Prepare for Future Contingencies, GAO-12-1026T, September 2012, p. 2.

[87] U.S. Government Accountability Office, Operational Contract Support: Management and Oversight Improvements Needed in Afghanistan, GAO-12-290, March 29, 2012, p. 17; Commission on Wartime Contracting In Iraq and Afghanistan, At What Risk? Correcting Over-reliance on Contractors in Contingency Operations, Second Interim Report to Congress, February 24, 2011, p. 26; Department of Defense, Initial Capabilities Document for Operational Contract Support, July 19, 2011, pp. 15-16, H-1. Section 845 of the National Defense Authorization Act for 2013 (P.L. 112-239) requires DOD to include operational contract support in Professional Military Education.

[88] Commission on Wartime Contracting In Iraq and Afghanistan, At What Risk? Correcting Over-reliance on Contractors in Contingency Operations, Second Interim Report to Congress, February 24, 2011, p. 26; Harvard Kennedy School, Transforming the National Security Culture, April 2009, p. 33; Office of the Undersecretary of Defense (AT&L), Improvements to Services Contracting, Report of the Defense Science Board Task Force, March 2011, p. 30; United States Institute of Peace, The QDR in Perspective: Meeting America's National Security Needs in the 21st Century, 2010, p. 39.

[89] Commission on Wartime Contracting In Iraq and Afghanistan, At What Risk? Correcting Over-reliance on Contractors in Contingency Operations, Second Interim Report to Congress, February 24, 2011, p. 27; U.S. Government Accountability Office, Defense Acquisitions: Tailored Approach Needed to Improve Service Acquisition Outcomes, GAO-07-20, November 9, 2006.

[90] Based on DOD documentation provided to CRS and discussions with DOD officials in Afghanistan, August-September 2011.

[91] U.S. Government Accountability Office, Operational Contract Support: Sustained Leadership Needed to Better Prepare for Future Contingencies, GAO-12-1026T, September 2012, p. 1; Commission on Wartime Contracting In Iraq and Afghanistan, Transforming Wartime Contracting: Controlling Costs, Reducing Risk, Final Report to Congress, August, 2011, p. 7.

[92] Commission on Wartime Contracting In Iraq and Afghanistan, At What Risk? Correcting Over-reliance on Contractors in Contingency Operations, Second Interim Report to Congress, February 24, 2011, p. 3.

[93] U.S. Government Accountability Office, Contingency Contracting: Observations on Actions Needed to Address Systemic Challenges, GAO-11-580, April 25, 2011, p. Highlights.

[94] Urgent Reform Required: Army Expeditionary Contracting, op cit., p. 7.

[95] U.S. Government Accountability Office. Military Operations: Contractors Provide Vital Services to Deployed Forces but Are Not Adequately Addressed in DOD Plans, GAO-03-695, June 2003, p. 36.

[96] Lieutenant Colonel Robert Gould, USA (Ret.), "Operational Contract Support: Not Just for Contingencies," Army Sustainment, July-August 2012, p. 24.

[97] Commission on Wartime Contracting In Iraq and Afghanistan, At What Risk? Correcting Over-reliance on Contractors in Contingency Operations, Second Interim Report to Congress, February 24, 2011, p. 25; U.S. Government Accountability Office, Operational Contract Support: Management and Oversight Improvements Needed in Afghanistan, GAO-12-290, March 29, 2012, p. 26; Lieutenant Colonel Robert Gould, USA (Ret.), "Operational Contract Support: Not Just for Contingencies," Army Sustainment, July-August 2012, p. 26.

[98] U.S. Government Accountability Office, Operational Contract Support: Management and Oversight Improvements Needed in Afghanistan, GAO-12-290, March 29, 2012, p. 17.

[99] Harvard Kennedy School, Transforming the National Security Culture, April 2009, p. 33; Office of the Undersecretary of Defense (AT&L), Improvements to Services Contracting, Report of the Defense Science Board Task Force, March 2011, p. 30; United States Institute of Peace, The QDR in Perspective: Meeting America's National Security Needs in the 21st Century, 2010, p. 39; Commission on Wartime Contracting In Iraq and Afghanistan, At What Risk? Correcting Over-reliance on Contractors in Contingency Operations, Second Interim Report to Congress, Second Interim Report to Congress, February 24, 2011, p. 3, 25; U.S. Government Accountability Office, Contingency Contracting: Observations on Actions Needed to Address Systemic Challenges, GAO-11-580, April 25, 2011, p. Highlights; Commission on Army Acquisition and Program Management in Expeditionary Operations, Urgent Reform Required: Army Expeditionary Contracting, October 31, 2007, page 55. This recommendation is also posited by the Center for New American Security.

[100] Joint Contingency Acquisition Support Office, Information Paper, "CRS Update to Reports on Operational Contract Support," February 7, 2013, p. 3; Commission on Wartime Contracting In Iraq and Afghanistan, At What Risk? Correcting Over-Reliance on Contractors in Contingency Operations, Second Interim Report to Congress, February 24, 2011; U.S. Government Accountability Office, Contingency Contracting: Observations on Actions Needed to Address Systemic Challenges, GAO-11-580, April 25, 2011.

[101] August 2011 in Kabul, Afghanistan.

[102] Professional Services Council, S. 2139 The Comprehensive Contingency Contracting Reform Act of 2012, Statement for the Record, April 17, 2012, p. 3.

[103] Commission on Wartime Contracting In Iraq and Afghanistan, Correcting Over-reliance on Contractors in Contingency Operations, Second Interim Report to Congress, February 24, 2011, p. Foreword; U.S. Government Accountability Office, Contingency Contracting: Observations on Actions Needed to Address Systemic Challenges, GAO-11-580, April 25, 2011, p. Highlights; U.S. Congress, Senate Committee on Homeland Security and Governmental Affairs, Ad Hoc Subcommittee on Contracting Oversight, The Comprehensive Contingency Contracting Reform Act of 2012 (S.2139), Statement for the Record of Katherine Schinasi, 112th Cong., 2nd sess., April 17, 2012, p. 1.

[104] Based on discussions with DOD officials, July 23, 2009.

[105] U.S. Government Accountability Office, Warfighter Support: DOD Needs Additional Steps to Fully Integrate Operational Support into Contingency Planning, GAO-13-212, February 2013, p. 22; U.S. Government Accountability Office, Contingency Contracting: Observations on Actions Needed to Address Systemic Challenges, GAO-11-580, April 25, 2011, p. 4.

[106] Commission on Wartime Contracting In Iraq and Afghanistan, Correcting Over-reliance on Contractors in Contingency Operations, Second Interim Report to Congress, February 24, 2011, p. 22.

[107] U.S. Government Accountability Office, Warfighter Support: DOD Needs Additional Steps to Fully Integrate Operational Support into Contingency Planning, GAO-13-212, February 2013, p. 22; based on discussions with DOD officials, June 2012. See also: U.S. Congress, Senate Committee on Homeland Security and Governmental Affairs, Ad Hoc Subcommittee on Contracting Oversight, The Comprehensive Contingency Contracting Reform Act of 2012 (S.2139), Testimony of Richard Ginman, Director, Defense Procurement and Acquisition Policy, Department of Defense, 112th Cong., 2nd sess., April 17, 2012, p. 12. According to CRS correspondence with DOD officials on April 30, 2013, "Based on GAO recommendations, DOD is taking action to provide operational planners with more detailed planning guidance for OCS. The Chairman of the Joint Chiefs of Staff is developing a manual specifically to assist in operational contract support planning. Tied to this effort, DOD is developing planning factors that enable the warfighter to conduct planning and estimate the contractor as well as the contracting component of the total force. Directly related to these specific actions, the Joint Staff is also developing a Joint OCS Planning and Execution Course (JOPEC) to enhance the planning skills and capabilities of OCS planners."

[108] CRS Report R41820, Department of Defense Trends in Overseas Contract Obligations, by Moshe Schwartz and Wendy Ginsberg; U.S. Government Accountability Office, Reliability of Federal Procurement Data, GAO-04-295R, December 30, 2003, p. 1. For an additional discussion on the importance of having reliable data to develop policies affecting acquisitions, see U.S. Government Accountability Office, Defense Acquisitions: Tailored Approach Needed to Improve Service Acquisition Outcomes, GAO-07-20, November 9, 2006.

[109] For a discussion on the importance of good contract data to improving government efficiency and saving taxpayer money, see U.S. Government Accounting Office, Opportunities to Reduce Potential Duplication in Government Programs, Save Tax Dollars, and Enhance Revenue: Collecting improved data on interagency contracting to minimize duplication could help the government leverage its vast buying power, GAO-11-318SP, March, 1, 2011, p. 70.

[110] Author's discussions with military officials and with contractors responsible for managing ISAF data, August-September, 2011. See also, See Report Regarding Contract Assessment

Among Donors and the Private Sector in Afghanistan, p. 15, which states "Due to a lack of reliable information, neither the Afghan government nor the international community can determine the amount of money spent in Afghanistan over the past 10 years."

111 General David H. Petraeus, Commander International Security Assistance Force/United States Forces-Afghanistan, Request to Establish a U.S. Government Acquisition Accountability Office for Afghanistan, United States Forces-Afghanistan, Memorandum, February 18, 2011, pp. 1-2.

112 U.S. Government Accountability Office, Iraq and Afghanistan: Availability of Forces, Equipment, and Infrastructure Should Be Considered in Developing U.S. Strategy and Plans, GAO-09-380T, February 12, 2009.

113 Author's discussions with military and civilian personnel in Kabul, Afghanistan August-September 2011, and on data indicating that in some areas, half of Contracting Officer's Representatives positions may be vacant. See also Commission on Wartime Contracting in Iraq and Afghanistan, At What Risk? Correcting Over-reliance on Contractors in Contingency Operations, Second Interim Report to Congress, February 24, 2011, p. 17; United States Institute of Peace, The QDR in Perspective: Meeting America's National Security Needs in the 21st Century, 2010, p. 39; U.S. Government Accountability Office, Military Operations: High-Level DOD Action Needed to Address Long-standing Problems with Management and Oversight of Contractors Supporting Deployed Forces, GAO-07-145, December 18, 2006; Commission on Wartime Contracting In Iraq and Afghanistan, Transforming Wartime Contracting: Controlling Costs, Reducing Risk, Final Report to Congress, August, 2011, p. 83-84.

114 Task Force 2010 Information Papers provided to CRS, dated May 8, 2011.

115 U.S. Army Audit Agency Office, Audit of Contracting Operations, Joint Contracting Command-Iraq/Afghanistan, Regional Contracting Center-Audit Report A-2010-0031-ALL, Memorandum, February 16, 2010, p. 2.

116 Department of Defense, Quadrennial Defense Review Report, February 2010, p. 77-78.

117 U.S. Congress, Senate Committee on Homeland Security and Governmental Affairs, Ad Hoc Subcommittee on Contracting Oversight, The Comprehensive Contingency Contracting Reform Act of 2012 (S.2139), Testimony of Richard Ginman, Director, Defense Procurement and Acquisition Policy, Department of Defense, 112th Cong., 2nd sess., April 17, 2012, p. 12-13.

118 Several recommendations made by the Commission on Wartime Contracting in Iraq and Afghanistan were adopted as provisions relating to wartime contracting in the National Defense Authorization Act for FY13 (P.L. 112-239).

119 For additional information on the Special Inspector for Afghanistan Reconstruction, see http://www.sigar.mil/.

120 The Special Inspector for Iraq Reconstruction was created by Congress in 2003 as the Office of the Inspector General of the Coalition Provisional Authority in order to provide for independent and objective conduct and supervision of audits and investigations relating to the programs and operations of the Coalition Provisional Authority. For a complete legislative history of the Special Inspector for Iraq Reconstruction, see http://www.sigir.mil/about/pub-law.html.

121 See http://www.acq.osd.mil/log/PS/p_vault/MOU_Signed_July2008.pdf. Section 854 of the National Defense Authorization Act for 2009 (P.L. 110-417) required agencies to modify this memorandum with information on offenses committed by or against contractor personnel, see http://www.acq.osd.mil/log/PS/p_vault/DOD_DOS_USAID_signature_20Apr2010.pdf.

[122] Updates Section 862 of the National Defense Authorization Act for 2008 (P.L. 110-181).

[123] Updates Section 832 of the National Defense Authorization Act for 2009 (P.L. 110-417).

[124] Section 515 of the National Defense Authorization Act for 2012 (P.L. 112-81) expanded the legal definition of 'contingency operation' (10 USC 101(a)(13)) by adding the following provision: "Authorizes the Secretary, upon request of a state governor for federal assistance in responding to a major disaster or emergency, to order a unit or member of the reserves to active duty for a continuous period of up to 120 days to provide such assistance. Excludes members so serving from reserve personnel end strength limits. Provides for the termination of such duty by order of the Secretary or by law. Requires the usual and customary command and control arrangement with respect to regular and reserve armed forces serving simultaneously in support of civil authorities during such a disaster or emergency."

[125] Updates 41 USC § 1702.

[126] Section 833 of the National Defense Authorization Act for 2009 (P.L. 110-417) authorized expedited hiring authority to fill shortages in the defense acquisition workforce through 2012; Section 833 of the National Defense Authorization Act for 2010 (P.L. 111-383) extended expedited hiring authority for defense acquisition workforce positions through 2015; and Section 803 of the National Defense Authorization Act for 2013 (P.L. 112-239) continued expedited hiring authority for defense acquisition workforce positions through 2017.

[127] Minimum data reporting elements required by Section 844 of the National Defense Authorization Act for 2013 (P.L. 112-239) are the following:

(1) The total number of contracts entered into as of the date of any report.

(2) The total number of such contracts that are active as of such date.

(3) The total value of contracts entered into as of such date.

(4) The total value of such contracts that are active as of such date.

(5) An identification of the extent to which the contracts entered into as of such date were entered into using competitive procedures.

(6) The total number of contractor personnel working under contracts entered into as of the end of each calendar quarter during the one-year period ending on such date.

(7) The total number of contractor personnel performing security functions under contracts entered into as of the end of each calendar quarter during the one-year period ending on such date.

(8) The total number of contractor personnel killed or wounded under any contracts entered into.

[128] Modifies Annual Joint Report and Comptroller Review on Contracting in Iraq in Afghanistan as required by Section 835 of the National Defense Authorization Act for 2011 (P.L. 111-383). See also Section 844 of the National Defense Authorization Act for 2013 (P.L. 112-239).

[129] Updates 41 USC §3312; see also Section 892 of the National Defense Authorization Act for 2011 (P.L. 111-383).

INDEX

D

E

F

G

H

I

J

K

L

M